THE DISTINGUISHED SERVICE CROSS

1901–1938

W. H. Fevyer

The London Stamp Exchange Ltd.

THE DISTINGUISHED SERVICE CROSS
1901–1938

FIRST PUBLISHED 1991 BY
THE LONDON STAMP EXCHANGE Ltd
The Naval & Military Book Specialists
5 BUCKINGHAM STREET, STRAND, LONDON WC2N 6BS

SET IN 9 POINT GARAMOND
LEADED 1 POINT
BY
LANGLANDS EDITION
LOUGHBOROUGH

Introduction

The Distinguished Service Cross traces its origin to the early days of this century when, in June 1901, the Conspicuous Service Cross was instituted. It was intended as a reward for Warrant Officers and Subordinate Officers, who by reason of not holding a Commission in the Royal Navy, were ineligible to receive any existing Order or Decoration. The design of the Cross, similar in outline to the Distinguished Service Order is classic in its simplicity. Bearing on the obverse the crowned monogram of the reigning monarch, the reverse is plain save for the London silver hallmarks. Shortly after the outbreak of the First World War, the Cross was re-designated 'The Distinguished Service Cross.' Eligibility was now extended to officers below the rank of Lieutenant-Commander, thus allowing reward for services that did not reach the required standard for the award of the D.S.O.

The D.S.C. will be known to most readers as an award for Naval Officers for gallant or distinguished services at sea. Yet, from the very inception of the C.S.C. in 1901, these Crosses have been awarded for a great variety of gallant acts performed on land and later in the air. Thus, we find that of the eight C.S.C.'s ever awarded, all but one were for services ashore. Similarly, during the First World War we see awards to Naval and Marine personnel serving with Armoured Cars in far away parts such as Armenia, Persia, Roumania and Turkey; with siege guns in France and Flanders; aboard Armoured Trains in North Russia against the Bolshevic Forces; and with the Royal Naval Air Service in virtually every theatre of war where an Allied presence was to be found. The large number of D.S.C.'s awarded for flying may be surprising but we must remember that until the formation of an independent Air Force in 1918 and the consequent introduction of new awards for that service, it was only appropriate that Naval airmen should receive a Naval Decoration.

Awards for services afloat or, indeed, submerged, also help to illustrate the incredible versatility of the Royal Navy at war. The picket boats of H.M. Ships 'Majestic' and 'Triumph' in an action reminiscent of the Boat Service actions of the Napoleonic Wars; the Coastal Motor Boats that attacked the Bolshevic fleet in Kronstadt harbour in one of the most audacious commando-style raids of the war; the two motor boats 'Mimi' and 'Toutou' that were hauled across Africa by oxen and steam traction engines to fight the German presence on Lake Tanganyika; the top secret 'Q' ships that became the scourge of every 'U' boat Commander and the boats of the submarine service that performed such gallant feats in the Sea of Marmora, the Baltic Sea and elsewhere.

We must not forget the men of the Merchant Navy who often found themselves embroiled in action with enemy ships, for their gallantry also was sometimes rewarded with the D.S.C. Nor, too, the fishermen of England who were to be found casting their nets across the Straits of Otranto in an effort to prevent enemy submarines leaving the Adriatic to harass our shipping in the Mediterranean.

Whilst the services for which the Cross was given were so varied, the actual numbers awarded were relatively few. For every D.S.C. awarded during the First World War, less than 2000 in total, there were 5 D.S.O.'s and 18 M.C.'s. That is not to say that the Royal Navy was hard done by, for the D.S.O. encompassed all the services and there were a great many more Officers in the Army by comparison. Nonetheless it remains a scarce award in the field of collecting today and is highly prized by collectors.

Within the pages of this book are recorded all recipients of the C.S.C. and D.S.C. as shown in the *London Gazette* for the period 1901-1938. Some awards to officers of allied Navies were not gazetted and are therefore not included. Nor too the award of the D.S.C. to the port of Dunkirk in 1919 which, perhaps, set the precedent for the award of the George Cross to the Island of Malta in 1942.

Whilst this information is not in itself new, it is for the first time presented in a single volume providing easy reference for collectors and historians alike. It will serve, above all, as a companion volume to 'The Distinguished Service Medal 1914-1920,' by the same compiler, and fill an important gap in every Naval Library.

Nimrod Dix,
London,
1990.

Recipients of the
Distinguished Service Cross
Late Conspicuous Service Cross
1901 – 1938

The KING has been graciously pleased to confer the decoration of the Conspicuous Service Cross on the following Warrant Officers and Subordinate Officers of the Royal Navy in recognition of their services during the operations in South Africa:—
LG 2.7.1901 p 4400

- Gunner Ernest Lowe.
  This Officer has performed the duty of Quartermaster to the Brigade while landed with untiring zeal and energy.
- Gunner Joseph Wright (also served on shore during the recent operations in China). Worked his guns well and was of great assistance in withdrawing them.
- Midshipman Thomas Charles Armstrong (now Acting Sub Lieutenant).
  Was with the guns and behaved with great gallantry in a very exposed position, which was commanded by the enemy's guns and where they were subjected to a heavy artillery fire, which proved so accurate as to wound six men of the guns crew.
- Midshipman Cymbeline Alonso Edric Huddart (killed in action)
  Behaved magnificently, and still advanced after he had been twice wounded until he was struck down mortally wounded.
- Midshipman Thomas Frederick John Livesey Wardle (Now Acting Sub Lieutenant).
  Showed great gallantry and remained with Major Plumbe and several dead and wounded men. Attended to them and dressed their wounds under a heavy fire.
- Midshipman Reginald Becher Caldwell Hutchinson.

His Majesty has been graciously pleased to confer the decoration of the Conspicuous Service Cross on Gunner George Mascull, Royal Navy, in recognition of his services during the operations in China.
LG 26.6.1902 p 4197

- Gunner George Mascull, R.N.
  Enclosure in Letter of Rear Admiral, China Station, dated 27th June 1900, No. 24. (*LG 5.10.1900*)

H.M.A. "Fame" Taku.
June 17th.

SIR,
IN compliance with your order of 16th instant to take H.M.S. "Whiting" under my command and capture the four Imperial Chinese destroyers lying between Taku and Tongku, so as to ensure the safe passage of the "Iltis", "German", and "Lion", French gun vessels at 3 a.m., I beg to report that having visited the place during the evening with Lieutenant and Commander Mackenzie of H.M.S. "Whiting", and found them moored head and stern in single line off the south steep-to bank with wire hawsers laid out from each bow and quarter, I arranged as follows:— That the "Fame" should weigh at 2 a.m. followed by the "Whiting" at a distance of about 1½ cables (the distance between the fourth and second destroyers). Each vessel to tow a whaler with a boarding party of 12 men under Lieutenants Tomlinson of H.M.S. "Fame" and Moreton of H.M.S. "Whiting". That we should pass well out in the stream to give them the idea we were proceeding up the river, and when the "Fame's" bow was abreast of No. 4 and the "Whiting's" abreast of No. 2, sheer in and board them over the bow, each whaler boarding the next astern, and each boarding party being covered by a rifle party and the guns.
When the forts commenced the heavy firing about 0.45, both ships being in a very exposed position and the necessity of clearing the river, immediate, I directed the "Whiting" to weigh and proceed as arranged. This was effected most successfully. After a slight resistance and the exchange of a few shots, the crews were driven overboard or below hatches; there were a few killed and wounded; our casualties nil. No damage was done to the prizes, the

"Fame's" bow was slightly bent when we closed to board, and the "Whiting" was struck by a projectile about 4 to 5 inches abreast a coal bunker. This was evidently fired from a mud battery on the bend between Taku and Tongku, which fired in all about 30 shots at us, none of the others striking, though several coming very close. I could not reply for fear of striking the Russian gunvessels lying behind it. There was a good deal of sniping from the dockyard, so I directed all cables of the prizes to be slipped and proceeded to tow them up to Tongku. At this point, Mr. Macrae, the manager of the "Tug and Lighter Company", came to my assistance; I cannot speak too highly of this gentleman's assistance, he took one destroyer off my hands, as did another of the same company's tugs for the "Whiting". In the former case Mr. Macrae had to use force, with the assistance of one of my men, on the Chinese crew, most of whom tried to jump overboard when we came under the fire of the mud battery. In the latter case, Mr. Mayne, Midshipman of the "Barfleur" was in command of a guard of seamen with a maxim, and also did very well. So soon as the destroyers were captured, the "Iltis" and "Lion" passed. The torpedoes were in the tubes, but war heads were not fitted. Ammunition for Q.F. guns in two destroyers was on deck.

By 5 a.m. they were securely berthed at Tongku. It was not a good position, owing to the exposure to shell passing over the bombarding ship, but the best I could find under the circumstances. Fortunately no damage was done.

Mr. Mayne, Midshipman in charge of a tug with despatches and stores for Tientsin informed me that his Chinese crew would not pass a fort 12 miles up the river at Lun Chang. So I proceeded in company with the "Whiting" to force a passage if necessary; finding no opposition I returned as directed by you to Taku.

Lieutenant Commander Mackenzie is forwarding a separate report. I can only say he did most excellently, as did Lieutenant Tomkinson in charge of the whaler boarding party, and Mr. Mascull, gunner, who took charge of the other destroyer. Mr. Knight, engineer, was of the greatest assistance in charge aft when I was left with a very small crew and no executive officer.

I have etc.
ROGER KEYES,
Lieutenant and Commander

The KING has been graciously pleased to confer the decoration of the Conspicuous Service Cross on Midshipman Arthur Gerald Onslow, Royal Navy, in recognition of his services during the operations in Somaliland. *LG 6.9.1904 p 5777*

● Midshipman Arthur Gerald Onslow, R.N.

The KING has been graciously pleased to give orders for the award of the Distinguished Service Cross (late Conspicuous Service Cross), in respect of the undermentioned Officers in recognition of their services mentioned in the foregoing despatches:—
LG 23.10.1914 p 8501

● Lieutenant Henry Edward Horan, H.M.S. "Liberty."
First Lieutenant who took command after the death of Lieutenant-Commander Barttelot, and brought his ship out of action in an extremely able and gallant manner under most trying conditions.

● Lieutenant Charles Manner Sutton Chapman, Second in Command H. M. Submarine E9.

● Lieutenant Charles Reid Peploe, H.M.S. "Laurel."
First Lieutenant, who took command after Commander Rose was wounded, and continued the action till its close, bringing his Destroyer out in an able and gallant manner under most trying conditions.

● Chief Gunner Ernest Roper, H.M.S. "Laforey." Carried out his duties with exceptional coolness under fire.

● Gunner Robert Mitchell Taylor, H.M.S. "Fearless."
For coolness in action under heavy fire.

● Gunner James Douglas Godfrey, H.M.S. "Arethusa."
In charge of torpedo tubes.

● Gunner Harry Morgan, H.M.S. "Liberty." Carried out his duties with exceptional coolness under fire.

● Acting Boatswain Charles Powell, H.M.S. "Laertes."
Who was gunlayer of the centre gun, which made many hits. He behaved very coolly, and set a good example when getting in tow and clearing away the wreckage after the action.

The following Memorandum has been furnished by the Admiral Commanding the East Coast Minesweepers, detailing the recent minesweeping operations off Scarborough.

From the 19th to the 31st December sweeping operations were conducted by the East Coast Minesweepers with the object of clearing the minefield which had been laid by the enemy off Scarborough.

At the beginning there was no indication of the position of the mines, although owing to losses of passing merchant ships it was known that a minefield had been laid.

In order to ascertain how the mines lay it was necessary to work at all times of tide with a consequent large increase in the element of danger.

The following officers are specially noticed for their services during the operations:—

Lieutenant C. V. Crossley, R.N.R., H.M.S. "Pekin". Whilst sweeping on 19th December, three violent explosions occurred close under the stern of his ship, Trawler No. 465 (Star of Britain). He controlled the crew, and himself crawled into a confined space near the screw shaft, discovered the damage, and temporarily stopped the leak sufficiently to enable the pumps to keep the water down and save the ship.

Skipper Thomas William Trendall, R.N.T.R., Trawler "Solon", No. 55, on his own responsibility went to the assistance of the Steamer "Gallier" which had just been mined on the night of 25th December. It was low water at the time and dark, and the "Gallier" was showing no lights, so had to be searched for in the mine field.

Skipper Ernest V. Snowline, R.N.T.R., Drifter "Hilda and Ernest" No. 201, carried out his duties as Commodore of the Flotilla of Lowestoft drifters under Chief Gunner Franklin, R.N. in a most satisfactory manner. He kept to his station in heavy weather, standing by the S.S. "Gallier" after she had been damaged by a mine.

The KING has been graciously pleased to give orders for the award of the Distinguished Service Cross in respect of the undermentioned Officers, in recognition of their services mentioned in the foregoing despatch:—
LG 19.2.1915 pp 1719/20

- Lieutenant C. V. Crossley, R.N.R.
- Skipper Thomas William Trendall, R.N.T.R.
- Skipper Ernest V. Snowline, R.N.T.R.

The KING has been graciously pleased to give orders for the Award of the Distinguished Service Cross in respect of the undermentioned Officers:—
LG 1.1.1915 p 5

- Lieutenant George Lionel Davidson, late His Majesty's Ship "Loyal".
- Lieutenant Gerald Gordon Grant, Royal Naval Volunteer Reserve, Royal Naval Division.
- Sub-Lieutenant Charles Oscar Frittriof Modin, Royal Naval Volunteer Reserve, Royal Naval Division.
- Lieutenant David James Gowney, Royal Marine Light Infantry, Royal Marine Brigade, Royal Naval Division.
- Lieutenant Harold Owen Joyce, late His Majesty's Ship "Vestal".
- Lieutenant Douglas Reid Kinnier, Royal Naval Reserve S.S. "Ortega".

The KING has been graciously pleased to award the Distinguished Service Cross to Lieutenant William Henry Propert, Royal Naval Reserve, of the Steamship "Laertes" for his gallant and spirited conduct in command of his unarmed ship when attacked by the gunfire and torpedo of an enemy submarine on the 10th February 1915.
LG 16.2.1915 p 1556

- Lieutenant William Henry Propert, R.N.R.

The KING has been graciously pleased to give orders for the award of the Distinguished Service Cross to the undermentioned Officers, in recognition of their services mentioned in the foregoing despatch. (Action which took place on 8th December 1914 against a German Squadron off the Falkland Islands. LG 3.3.1915 pp 2207/9):—
LG 3.3.1915 p 2210

- Carpenter Thomas Andrew Walls, H.M.S. "Invincible".
- Carpenter William Henry Venning, H.M.S. "Kent".
- Carpenter George Henry Egford, H.M.S. "Cornwall".

The KING has been graciously pleased to give orders for the award of the Distinguished Service Cross, to the undermentioned Officers in recognition of their services mentioned in the foregoing despatch. (Action in the North Sea on Sunday 24th January 1915):—
LG 3.3.1915 p 2213

- Surgeon Probationer James Alexander Stirling, R.N.V.R.
- Gunner (T) Joseph H. Burton
- Chief Carpenter Frederick E. Dailey.

The KING has been graciously pleased to award the Distinguished Service Cross to the undermentioned Officers:—
LG 19.3.1915 p 2737

- Lieutenant Denys Charles Gerald Shoppee, Royal Navy, for gallant and distinguished service in the field.
- Lieutenant John William Bell, Royal Naval Reserve, of the steamship "Thordis" for his gallant and spirited conduct in ramming a German submarine, which had fired a torpedo at the "Thordis", on the 28th February 1915.

The KING has been graciously pleased to approve of the award of the Distinguished Service Cross to the following Officer in recognition of his gallant and resolute conduct when the steamship "Vosges", of which he was in command was attacked by a German submarine on the 27th March 1915:—
LG 9.4.1915 p 3448

- Lieutenant John Richard Green, Royal Naval Reserve.

The KING has been graciously pleased to give orders for the award of the Distinguished Service Cross to the undermentioned Officers in recognition of their services as mentioned:—
LG 10.4.1915 p 3550

For services in the action between H.M.S. "Carmania" and the German Armed Merchant Cruiser, "Cap Trafalgar", on 14th September 1914 when the latter vessel was sunk:—
- Chief Gunner Henry Middleton
- Acting Sub-Lieutenant George Frederick Dickens, R.N.R.
- Midshipman (now Acting Sub-Lieutenant) Douglas Nowell Colson, R.N.R.

For services during the operations at Dar-es-Salaam on the 28th November 1914 when boats' parties from H.M.S. "Fox" and "Goliath" were attacked unexpectedly at the harbour entrance:—
- Lieutenant Eric Reid Corson, R.N.
- Lieutenant Herbert Walter Julian Orde, R.N.
- Sub-Lieutenant Clement James Charlewood, R.N.R.

Lieutenant Corson was in H.M.S. "Fox's" steam cutter and under a close and heavy fire from both sides of the channel, climbed forward to relieve a stoker who was mortally wounded. By his exertions he kept the fires going and steam up at the most critical moment.
Lieutenant Orde was in H.M.S. "Helmuth" and, though himself wounded and under exceptionally heavy fire, with dangerous escape of steam, brought his ship safely through the narrow channel.
Sub-Lieutenant Charlewood ably assisted Lieutenant Orde in bringing the "Helmuth" through the channel.

For services in H.M.S. "Hardinge" during the operations on the Suez Canal, 3rd February 1915:—
- Temporary Lieutenant George Carew, R.N.R. A shell struck the fore funnel of H.M.S. "Hardinge", and completely shattered one of Lieutenant Carew's legs from the knee down, and broke one arm, besides inflicting other wounds. Notwithstanding this, he continued to advise on the piloting of the ship with coolness and equanimity.

The KING has been graciously pleased to approve of the award of the Distinguished Service Cross to the undermentioned Officers of Submarine E.14:—
LG 21.5.1915 p 4894

- Lieutenant Edward Geldard Stanley, Royal Navy.
- Acting Lieutenant Reginald Wilfred Lawrence, Royal Naval Reserve.

The KING has been graciously pleased to give orders for the award of the Distinguished Service Cross to Flight Lieutenant John Philip Wilson, R.N. and Flight Sub-Lieutenant John Stanley Mills, R.N. for their services on the 7th June 1915, when, after a long flight in the darkness over hostile territory they threw bombs on the Zeppelin shed at St. Evere, near Brussels, and destroyed a Zeppelin, which was inside. The two Officers were exposed to heavy fire from anti-aircraft guns during the attack.
LG 22.6.1915 p 6020

- Flight Lieutenant John Phillip Wilson, R.N.
- Flight Sub-Lieutenant John Stanley Mills, R.N.

The KING has been graciously pleased to give orders for the award of the Distinguished Service Cross in respect of the undermentioned Officers, in recognition of their services with the Mediterranean Expeditionary Force:—
LG 3.6.1915 p 5331

- Lieutenant Ernest G. Boissier, Royal Naval Volunteer Reserve, Howe Battalion, Royal Naval Division.

- Lieutenant James Cheetham, Royal Marine Light Infantry, Chatham Battalion, Royal Marine Brigade, Royal Naval Division.
- Lieutenant George Spence Davidson, Royal Naval Volunteer Reserve, Anson Battalion, Royal Naval Division.

With reference to the list of awards to Officers and men of the Royal Naval Division in recognition of their services with the Mediterranean Expeditionary Force, which appeared in the *London Gazette* of the 3rd June 1915, the following are statements of the services of the Officers and men therein mentioned:—
LG 2.7.1915 p 6436

Lieutenant Ernest G. Boissier, Royal Naval Volunteer Reserve.
Behaved with gallantry in charge of a machine gun on May 7th, during operations South of Achi Baba, and effected the destruction of an enemy machine gun.
Lieutenant James Cheetham, Royal Marine Light Infantry.
Conducted himself with gallantry on May 1st during operations South of Achi Bab. When the enemy in strength of about a Battalion, attacked an outpost of 30 men. Lieutenant Cheetham called for two volunteers, and dashing out to a flank under heavy fire into the open, brought rapid fire to bear on the enemy and thus checked the attack and saved the outpost line.
Lieutenant George S. Davidson, Royal Naval Volunteer Reserve. Displayed great courage and coolness in action on May 6th during operations South of Achi Baba.

The KING has been graciously pleased to approve of the grant of the Victoria Cross to Lieutenant Commander Martin Eric Nasmith, Royal Navy, for the conspicuous bravery specified below:—

Lieutenant Commander Martin Eric Nasmith, Royal Navy
For most conspicuous bravery in command of one of His Majesty's Submarines while operating in the Sea of Marmora. In the face of great danger he succeeded in destroying one large Turkish gunboat, two transports, one ammunition ship and three storeships, in addition to driving one storeship ashore. When he had safely passed the most difficult part of his homeward journey he returned again to torpedo a Turkish transport.

The KING has been graciously pleased to approve of the award of the Distinguished Service Cross to the undermentioned Officers of the same Submarine:—
LG 25.6.1915 p 6166

- Lieutenant Guy D'Oyly-Hughes, Royal Navy.
- Acting Lieutenant Robert Brown, Royal Naval Reserve.

The KING has been graciously pleased to give orders for the following award of the Distinguished Service Cross to the under-mentioned Officer in recognition of his services as mentioned:—
LG 30.6.1915 pp 6355/6

For services while attached to landing parties from H.M.S. "Doris" on the Syrian Coast.—
- Lieutenant H. Pirie Gordon, R.N.V.R.
This Officer has been specially mentioned for bravery under fire by the Commander in Chief East Indies.
The Commanding Officer of H.M.S. "Doris" reports:—
With regard to the Officers who have taken part in the landing parties, I should like particularly to bring to notice the name of Lieutenant H. Pirie Gordon, R.N.V.R., who has landed on every occasion, and whose conduct has gained my highest approval at all times.

For services in the operations off Smyrna, 8th March 1915, when HM Minesweeper 285 was sunk by a mine:—
- Skipper James Sargent, R.N.R.
Skipper Sargent was in the armoured wheel-house when the explosion occurred, and, although severely bruised by a heavy iron plate, picked his way to the after end of the shattered and sinking vessel with the object of ordering Second Engineman F. W. Ingram to stop the engines, the engine room telegraph being broken. He continued to encourage his men and did not leave the vessel until she sank beneath him.

For services in connection with minesweeping operations in the Dardanelles:—
- Skipper Alfred Swain, R.N.R.
- Skipper Alfred E. Berry, R.N.R.

For meritorious service in connection with the sinking of the German Cruiser "Dresden", 14th March 1915:—
- Lieutenant Charles Gage Stuart, R.N.

For meritorious service in the North Sea:—
- Lieutenant Herbert James Ferguson, R.N.R.
- Skipper John Cowie, R.N.R.

For services in connection with the attack on the Austrian Monitors, 21st and 22nd April 1915:—

- Gunner (Acting) William Long, R.N.
  Mr. Long fired the torpedo which exploded against the enemy's Monitor and is believed to have sunk her.

The KING has been graciously pleased to give orders for the award of the Distinguished Service Cross to the undermentioned Officers in recognition of their services in the Patrol Cruisers since the outbreak of war:—
LG 6.8.1915 p 7849

- Lieutenant Samuel Bolton, R.N.R.
- Lieutenant Bernard Herbert Symns, R.N.R.
- Lieutenant Percy Reginald Vaughan, R.N.R.
- Lieutenant (Acting) Herbert Spencer, R.N.R.
- Lieutenant (Acting) Charles Walter Cartwright, R.N.R.
- Lieutenant (Acting) Edwin Alexander Stuart, R.N.R.
- Lieutenant (Acting) Robert Hobson, R.N.R.
- Warrant Telegraphist Samuel Lemon, R.N.R.

The KING has been graciously pleased to give orders for the award of the Distinguished Service Cross to the following Officers:—
LG 7.8.1915 p 7850

- Lieutenant Ion Beauchamp Butler Tower, R.N.
  For conspicuous coolness and bravery in charge of a naval gun on shore in Belgium, when subjected to heavy and accurate fire from hostile artillery on the 28th April 1915.
- Sub-Lieutenant Arthur Henry Seymour Casswell, R.N.
  For conspicuous coolness and gallantry on the 28th April 1915, when in charge of a naval gun on shore in Belgium, in removing ammunition from a burning building under heavy and well directed fire.
- Lieutenant Frederick Henry Taylor, R.N.
- Sub-Lieutenant (now Lieutenant) Charles Thomas Nettleingham, R.N.R.

The KING has been graciously pleased to give orders for the award of the Distinguished Service Cross to the undermentioned Officers, in recognition of their services, as mentioned in the foregoing despatch. (Gallipoli Landings, 25th to 26th April 1915. LG 16.8.1915 pp 8125/9):—
LG 16.8.1915 p 8132

- Lieutenant Mass Goolden, R.N., H.M.S. "Prince of Wales".

- Boatswain John Murphy, R.N., H.M.S. "Cornwallis".
- Midshipman Rupert Edward Maximilian Bethune, R.N., H.M.S. "Inflexible".
- Midshipman Eric Oloff de Wet, R.N., H.M.S. "London".
- Midshipman Charles Wilfred Croxford, R.N.R., H.M.S. "Queen"
- Midshipman Cecil Aubrey Lawson Mansergh, R.N., H.M.S. "Queen".
- Midshipman Alfred Martyn Williams, R.N., H.M.S. "Euryalus".
- Midshipman Hubert Malcolm Wilson, R.N., H.M.S. "Euryalus".
- Midshipman George Francis Dudley Freer, R.N., H.M.S. "Lord Nelson".
- Midshipman Richard Victor Symonds-Taylor, R.N., H.M.S. "Agamemnon"
- Midshipman Cecil Hugh Clinton Matthey, R.N., H.M.S. "Queen Elizabeth".
- Midshipman John Saville Metcalf, R.N.R., H.M.S. "Triumph".

The KING has been graciously pleased to give orders for the award of the Distinguished Service Cross to the undermentioned Officers in recognition of their services as mentioned:—
LG 16.8.1915 pp 8133/4

- Sub-Lieutenant (now Acting Lieutenant) Stephen Augustus Bayford, R.N.R., H.M.S. "Majestic".
- Midshipman James Charles Woolmer Price, H.M.S. "Ocean".
  These officers were both in command of picket boats on night of 13th-14th March. When "Ocean's" boat lay helpless, having been struck in the boiler room by a shell, "Majestic" took her in tow, under heavy fire, the conduct of these two young officers being altogether admirable, as was their handling of their boats.
- Gunner (T) John William Alexander Chubb, R.N.
  Mr. Chubb, when a volunteer in trawler No. 488, on the night of 13th-14th March, brought his vessel out of action in a sinking condition, his commanding officer and three of the small crew being killed.
- Gunner (T) William Walter Thorrowgood, R.N.
  Mr. Thorrowgood was in command of an armed whaler which, on night of 4th-5th March, twice went into the shore between Kum Kale and Yeni Shehr, bringing off two officers and five men, two of them wounded, exposed to rifle fire on both occasions.
- Midshipman Hugh Dixon, R.N.
  Midshipman Dixon was in command of "Queen Elizabeth's" picket boat, and was

responsible for saving several officers and men from "Irresistible" while under heavy fire on the 18th March.

- Acting Sub-Lieutenant (now Sub-Lieutenant) George Tothill Philip, R.N.
  Acting Sub-Lieutenant Philip, H.M.S. "Inflexible" was in charge of his picket boat on the 18th March to deal with floating mines. The picket boat was struck by a heavy shell. Acting Sub-Lieutenant Philip got her alongside "Inflexible", ordered his crew inboard, and, though his knee was injured, got into the engine room, shut off steam and closed scuttle to stokehold before leaving his boat.
- Lieutenant Arthur Cyril Brooke-Webb, R.N.R.
- Midshipman John Blaxland Woolley, R.N.
  These officers took part in the picket boat attack on the 18th April.
- Lieutenant Colin George MacArthur, R.N.
  Lieutenant MacArthur (commanding submarine B6) carried out two most enterprising reconnaissances of E15, both under fire. During the latter reconnaissance his skilful handling saved his ship.

The KING has been graciously pleased to give orders for the award of the Distinguished Service Cross to the following Officers:—
LG 13.9.1915 pp 9064/5

- Lieutenant Colin Cantlie, R.N.
- Lieutenant Irving Montgomery Palmer, R.N.
  For his services in command of H.M.S. "Comet" during the advance on Amara, where he was landed with a very small force to preserve order, and at the barracks though accompanied by only two men, he received the surrender of a battalion of Turkish officers and men.
- Sub-Lieutenant Reginald Horace Lilley, R.N.
  For his services in charge of a 4.7" gun in a horseboat, and for the excellent manner in which he performed the difficult and dangerous task of securing a small steam tug, which had been left at Amara by the enemy with steam up, with a large lighter alongside her, and shipping in the lighter about 80 officers and 800 men who had been taken prisoners. Many of these had to be disarmed, and Sub-Lieutenant Lilley had only two men to assist him in the task.
- Acting Lieutenant Alan Bennis Fennel Alcock, R.M.L.I., Portsmouth Battalion.
  For gallantry and good service near Gaba Tepe, between the 28th April and 1st May, 1915. Accompanied by Lieutenant Empson, of the same regiment, with two platoons, numbering in all 60 men, he defended an isolated trench against overwhelming odds. Lieutenant Empson

was wounded early in the day on April 30th, and was killed on May 1st, and Lieutenant Alcock was finally compelled to withdraw, after having held this ground for four nights and three days. During this time no food or water could be conveyed to the trench, and at one time ammunition was reduced to about 15 rounds per man.

- Lieutenant George Swinney, R.N.R.
- Lieutenant John Thomas Randell, R.N.R.
- Lieutenant Thomas Edward Price, R.N.R.
- Lieutenant Francis William Lyte, R.N.R.
  For his services as pilot of the armed launch "Shushan", on the 9th May 1915, when he handled the vessel with the utmost coolness under fire. Lieutenant Lyte has done good work in the Shatt-el-Arab operations on many other occasions.
- Sub-Lieutenant Charles James Gibbon, R.N.R.
- Sub-Lieutenant Charles Henry Hudson, R.N.R.
- Acting Sub-Lieutenant Irvine Muirhead Twyman, R.N.R.
  For his services in the submarine commanded by Lieutenant-Commander Cochrane in the Sea of Marmora.
- Sub-Lieutenant Frederick Parslow, R.N.R.
  For his services in the horse-transport "Anglo-Californian", which was attacked by a German submarine on the 4th July and subjected to heavy gun fire for an hour and a half. Sub-Lieutenant Parslow steered the ship throughout the action and maintained his post after his father, the Captain of the ship, had been killed by a shell, until some of our patrol boats arrived and drove the submarine off.
- Engineer James Crawford, R.N.R.
  For his services as Chief Engineer of the same transport, in the escape of which he was largely instrumental by maintaining the vessel's maximum speed in spite of a shortage of firemen.
- Skipper Jesse Jones, R.N.R.
- Skipper Albert Edward Sayers, R.N.R.
- Monsieur le Lieutenant de vasseau Henry Julien Paul de l'Escaille, de la Marine francaise.
  For his services in command of the French Seaplane Squadron in Egypt. During the earlier part of this year, when hostile patrols were in touch with the Allied forces holding the Suez Canal, Lieutenant de vaisseau de l'Escaille, as pilot, made some brilliant and daring recon-naissances over long stretches of the Sinai Peninsula, where engine failure meant certain destruction to plane and to pilot. On these occasions, although under fire, by his skill and courage, he never failed to secure valuable information as to the enemy's movements.

- Monsieur le Lieutenant de vasseau Alfred Louis Marie Cintré, de la Marine francaise.
  For his services as a seaplane pilot in Egypt. He displayed great skill and intrepidity in a reconnaissance over Bir Saba on the 11th April 1915, when his plane was subjected to a heavy shrapnel and musketry fire, and was hit in more than once place. With consummate coolness Lieutenant de vasseau Cintré circled over Bir Saba again and again, until the number and position of the enemy were observed. He then turned his plane towards the ship, and, though the engine was damaged, succeeded by very skilful handling in traversing the distance of thirty five miles to the coastline in safety.

The KING has been pleased to approve of the award of the Distinguished Service Cross to the undermentioned officers of the Royal Naval Division in recognition of their services in the Gallipoli Peninsula:—
LG 8.11.1915 p 11029

- Lieutenant John Bigelow Dodge, R.N.V.R.
- Surgeon John Pratt, R.N.
- Lieutenant Ernest Horace Lamb, R.M.
- Lieutenant Murdoch Campbell Browne, R.M.
- Lieutenant Ronald Howarth Roe, R.M.

The KING has been graciously pleased to give orders for the award of the Distinguished Service Cross to the undermentioned Officers:—
LG 19.11.1915 p 11558

- Lieutenant Godfrey Craik Parsons, R.N.
  In recognition of his consistently gallant behaviour, whilst engaged in minesweeping operations, and particularly on the 4th September 1915, when, the vessel in which he was serving having struck a mine and Lieutenant Parsons himself having been crippled by severe wounds, he nevertheless crawled from the bridge to the boat deck to obtain assistance for another Officer who was lying unconscious on the bridge.
- Lieutenant Charles Edward Hamond, R.N.
- Lieutenant Cuthbert Helsham Heath-Caldwell, R.N.
  For services during the operations in Mesopotamia. Lieutenant Heath-Caldwell has been in command of the armed launch "Miner", and has handled his ship with skill when under fire on many occasions.
- Lieutenant Fitzadam Millar, R.N.
  For services in command of a naval detachment on shore at Aden.

- Lieutenant Hugh Fortescue Curry, R.N.
  For his services in command of the stern wheel steamer, "Muzaffri" on the 24th July, 1915, when he landed a supply of ammunition for the troops on the right bank of the Euphrates under heavy fire from the Turkish guns.
- Lieutenant William Vesey Hamilton Harris, R.N.
  For his services in command of the armed launch Sumana on the 24th July 1915, when he behaved with great gallantry under very heavy gun and rifle fire while placing a barge across the Mejenineh creek to bridge it for the troops.
- Captain George Carpenter, R.M.L.I.
- Lieutenant Edward Albert Singeisen, R.N.R.
  For services during landing operations in the Persian Gulf in August 1915.
- Lieutenant James Cadman, R.N.V.R.
  For coolness and daring in charge of armoured cars under very severe shell and shrapnel fire from May 12th to 14th, 1915.
- Engineer John Munro Dowie, R.N.R.
- Gunner Ernest Martin Jehan, R.N.
- Mr. James George Law, Gunner T, R.N.
  For services in charge of the mining launch employed in the Serbian rivers.
- Acting Boatswain Thomas Tierney, R.N.
  For services during landing operations in the Persian Gulf in August 1915.

The KING has been graciously pleased to give orders for the award of the Distinguished Service Cross to the undermentioned Officer in recognition of his services and signal gallantry in charge of machine guns in the Gallipoli Peninsula:—
LG 17.12.1915 p 12561

- Lieutenant Theodore Douglas Hallam, R.N.V.R. (now Acting Flight-Lieutenant, R.N.).

The KING has been graciously pleased to confer the undermentioned rewards on Officers and Men of the French Navy, with the approval of the President of the Republic, in recognition of their bravery and distinguished service in the campaign:—
LG 23.12.1915 p 12794

- Le Lieutenant de Vaisseau Paul Marie Joseph Blanc, Commandant de Dragueurs aux Dardanelles.
- Le Lieutenant de Vaisseau Jacques Lucien Boissarie, Commandant de Dragueurs aux Dardanelles.
- Le Lieutenant de Vaisseau Charles Francois Henri Ronzaud, Commandant de Dragueurs aux Dardanelles.

- Le Lieutenant de Vaisseau Louis Théophile Litré, Commandant de Dragueurs aux Dardanelles.
- Le Lieutenant de Vaisseau Jules Bergeon, Commandant de Dragueurs aux Dardanelles.
- Le Lieutenant de Vaisseau Maurice Alphonse Thierry, Commandant de Dragueurs aux Dardanelles.
- Le Lieutenant de Vaisseau Marie Achille Edouard Pierre Auverney, Commandant de Dragueurs aux Dardanelles.
- Le Lieutenant de Vaisseau Emile Victor Faurie, Commandant de Dragueurs aux Dardanelles.
- L'Officier de 2e Classe des Equipages de la Flotte Yves Louis Sergent, Commandant de Dragueurs aux Dardanelles.
- Le Lieutenant de Vaisseau Charles Lucien Cantener, de la Brigade des Fusiliers-Marins.
- Le Lieutenant de Vaisseau Robert Louis Marie Cayrol, de la Brigade des Fusiliers-Marins.
- Le Lieutenant de Vaisseau Siméon Marie Robert de Roucy, de la Brigade des Fusiliers-Marins.
- Le Lieutenant de Vaisseau Louis Octave Edouard Thévenard, du "Bouvet".
- Le Lieutenant de Vaisseau Eugène Marie Joseph Morris, du "Suffren".
- Le Lieutenant de Vaisseau Julien Joseph Perrette, du "Gaulois".
- Le Lieutenant de Vaisseau Charles Marie Joseph Millot, à la disposition de l'Amirauté britannique.
- Le Lieutenant de Vaisseau Joseph Henry Pierre de Bronac de Vazelhes, à la disposition de l'Amirauté britannique.
- Le Lieutenant de Vaisseau Vincent August de Pianelli, Commandant le "Francis-Garnier".
- Le Lieutenant de Vaisseau Louis Marie Jules Barthélemy de Saizieu, de l'Aviation Maritime.
- Le Lieutenant de Vaisseau Eugène Robert Defforges, Commandant le Bernouilli.
- Le Lieutenant de Vaisseau Jean Marie Michel Delègue, Commandant le "Coulomb".
- Le Lieutenant de Vaisseau John Pierre Esteva, à la base de Mudros.
- Le Lieutenant de Vaisseau Gustave de Peytes de Montcabrier, Etat-Major du Corps Expéditionnaire d'Orient.
- Le Lieutenant de Vaisseau de Réserve Marie Chrétien Galiot Martial Antonin de Mandat de Grancey, détaché au Grand Quartier Général des troupes anglaises.
- Le Lieutenant de Vaisseau Edmond David Willm, du "Montcalm".
- Le Lieutenant de Vaisseau Constant Charles René Bonnin, Commandant la "Fanfare".

- Le Lieutenant de Vaisseau Louis Paul Noël Marie Rouault de Coligny, Commandant la "Sabretache".
- L'Enseigne de Vaisseau de Réserve Gaston Ernest Maurice Dunoyer de Noirmont, détaché au Grand Quartier Général des troupes anglaises.
- L'Enseigne de Vaisseau auxiliaire Léon Gabriel Corblet, détaché au Grand Quartier Général des troupes anglaises.

The KING has been graciously pleased to approve of the grant of the Victoria Cross to Squadron Commander Richard Bell Davies, DSO, R.N., and of the Distinguished Service Cross to Flight Sub-Lieutenant Gilbert Formby Smylie, R.N., in recognition of their behaviour in the following circumstances:—

On the 19th November these two officers carried out an air attack on Ferrijik Junction. Flight Sub-Lieutenant Smylie's machine was received by very heavy fire and brought down. The pilot planed down over the station, releasing all his bombs except one, which failed to drop, simultaneously at the station from a very low altitude. Thence he continued his descent into the marsh. On alighting he saw the one unexploded bomb, and set fire to his machine, knowing that the bomb would ensure its destruction. He then proceeded towards Turkish territory.
At this moment he perceived Squadron-Commander Davies descending, and fearing that he would come down near the burning machine and thus risk destruction from the bomb, Flight Sub-Lieutenant Smylie ran back and from a short distance exploded the bomb by means of a pistol bullet. Squadron-Commander Davies descended at a safe distance from the burning machine, took up Sub-Lieutenant Smylie, in spite of the near approach of a party of the enemy, and returned to the aerodrome, a feat of airmanship that can seldom have been equalled for skill and gallantry.
LG 1.1.1916 p 86.

- Flight Sub-Lieutenant Gilbert Formby Smylie, R.N.

The KING has been graciously pleased to give orders for the award of the Distinguished Service Cross to the undermentioned Officers in recognition of their bravery and devotion to duty during minesweeping and mine-laying operations:—
LG 1.1.1916. p 86.

- Lieutenant Humphrey John Lancaster, R.N.
- Lieutenant Robert Jardine Carruthers, R.N.V.R.
- Sub-Lieutenant Alexander Daniells, R.N.R.
- Sub-Lieutenant George Gordon Rose, R.N.R.
- Sub-Lieutenant William Quinn McKeown, R.N.R.
- Sub-Lieutenant Harry Beedle, R.N.R.
- Gunner (T) Arthur Samuel Edmund Roberts, R.N.
- Artificer-Engineer Arthur Lewis Shaw, R.N.
- Skipper Frederick Wink, R.N.R.
- Skipper Francis McPherson, R.N.R.

The KING has been graciously pleased to give orders for the award of the Distinguished Service Cross to the undermentioned Officers:—
LG 1.1.1916 p 89.

- Lieutenant Ralph Daniel Blyth Haddon, R.N.
For his services during operations in the Cameroons. Lieutenant Haddon behaved with great gallantry when in command of H.M.S. "Cumberland's" picket boat during the attacks on Jabassi on the 8th and 14th October, 1914, when he was frequently under fire of the enemy's maxims at close range. On the 27th November 1914 during a reconnaissance with two motor launches near Jabassi, the native crews left their posts on coming under a heavy fire, whereupon Lieutenant Haddon, with Midshipman H. Beckett Anderson, R.N., and Richard R. Beauchamp, R.N., continued to manoeuvre the launches and engage the enemy with maxims for fifty minutes, finally silencing them.
- Lieutenant Arthur William Lancelot Brewill, R.N.
For his services in command of a naval gun on shore in Flanders.
- Captain (now Major) George Leonard Raikes, R.M.A.
For services with the Royal Marine Artillery Heavy Howitzer Brigade in France.
- Captain William Noel Stokes, R.M.A.
For services with the Army Ordnance Department in France.
- Captain George Pinckard Lathbury, R.M.L.I.
For services with the Royal Naval Division in Gallipoli, where he performed exceptionally good services with the machine guns of the Royal Marine Brigade, and showed coolness and resource on critical occasions.
- Temporary Captain Frank Summers, R.M.
For services with the Royal Naval Division Motor Transport Company in France.
- Acting Lieutenant Harold Roger Lambert, R.M.

For services with the Royal Marine Artillery Anti-Aircraft Brigade in France.
- Temporary lieutenant Thomas Cuming, R.M.
For services with the Royal Marine Artillery Heavy Howitzer Brigade in France.
- Acting Lieutenant Francis Cecil Law, R.M.
For his services with the Royal Naval Division in Gallipoli, where by his behaviour at a critical moment he stopped a retirement.
- Midshipman Hugh Beckett Anderson, R.N.
For his services during operations in the Cameroons. On the 9th December, 1914, during a reconnaissance in a motor launch towards Jabassi Midshipman Anderson's maxim jambed while he was returning the fire of the enemy, who were engaging him from both banks. Mr. Anderson not only handled his boat well, but personally cleared his maxim under a continuous heavy fire, and then swept both banks with it, the enemy suffering heavily.

Mr. L. Scarlett, Skipper, R.N.R., HM Drifter "Hyacinth".
On 25th September, off Zeebrugge exhibited great coolness in action, remaining and completing his task though exposed to heavy gun fire.
Lieutenant L. F. Robinson, H.M.S. Lord Clive.
Gunnery Lieutenant of "Lord Clive", the excellent shooting of which ship has contributed materially to the damage done.

His Majesty the KING has been graciously pleased to give orders for the award of the Distinguished Service Cross to the under-mentioned Officers in recognition of their services as mentioned in the foregoing despatch. (Dover patrol, off Belgian Coast, 22nd August to 19th November 1915. *LG 12.1.1916 pp 545/7):*
LG 12.1.1916 pp 547/8

- Lieutenant Lionel Frederick Robinson, R.N.
- Skipper Lawrence Scarlett, R.N.R.

The KING has been graciously pleased to give orders for the award of the Distinguished Service Cross to the undermentioned Officers in recognition of their services during the advance on Kut-el-Amara on the 27th and 28th September 1915:—
LG 21.1.1916 pp 943/4

- Flight Lieutenant Vivian Gaskell Blackburn, R.N.
Flight Lieutenant Blackburn did excellent air reconnaissance work, and came under heavy fire on the afternoon of the 28th September

whilst carrying despatches between the General Officer Commanding and the "Comet".

- Surgeon Dermot Loughlin, M.B., R.N.
  Surgeon Loughlin attended the wounded on board the "Comet" under a heavy fire at close quarters on the night of the 28th September.
- Engineer Thomas Kerr, R.I.M.
  Engineer Kerr not only kept the Lascar engine-room complement of the "Comet" in excellent order during action, but assisted in carrying down the wounded under fire.
- Sub-Lieutenant Lionel Charles Paul Tudway, R.N.
  Sub Lieutenant Tudway was in command of the armed launch "Sumana", and showed remarkable ability and coolness in manoeuvring his vessel under heavy fire on the night of the 28th September, and on several other occasions under fire.

The KING has been graciously pleased to approve of the award of the Distinguished Service Cross to the undermentioned Officers:—
LG 24.2.1916 pp 2077/8

- Surgeon Alfred Robinson MacMullin, R.N.
  For his services on the 23rd January 1916, at Serengeti, in East Africa, when he showed remarkable bravery in searching for and rescuing a severely wounded officer under heavy machine gun and rifle fire close to concealed enemy entrenchments.
- Captain Dudley Leigh Aman, R.M.A.
  For his services with the Royal Marine Artillery Anti-Aircraft Brigade. Captain Aman has commanded two sections of anti-aircraft guns in the salient of Ypres continuously since the 3rd May 1915, with marked success and has shown great ability and zeal, and a fine example of coolness and courage under fire.
- Temporary Captain Guy Evans, R.M.
  For his services with the Royal Marine Artillery Anti-Aircraft Brigade. Captain Evans has commanded a section of anti-aircraft guns in the Salient of Ypres continously since the 12th May 1915, and has shown an example of conspicuous coolness and courage on every occasion under the continual conditions of fire to which the section has been exposed.
- Flight Sub-Lieutenant Arthur Strachan Ince, R.N.
  For his services as observer and gunner on the 14th December 1915, when with Flight Sub-Lieutenant Graham he attacked and destroyed a German seaplane off the Belgian coast.

The KING has been graciously pleased to approve of the award of the Distinguished Service Cross to Acting Lieutenant Francis Tweedie, R.N.R.
LG 7.3.1916 p 2459

- Acting Lieutenant Francis Tweedie, R.N.R.

The KING has been graciously pleased to approve of the award of the Distinguished Service Cross to the undermentioned Officers:—
LG 14.3.1916 pp 2870/1

- Lieutenant Eric Ritchie Bent, R.N.
  Has performed consistent good work as Naval Observation Officer on shore from the first days of the landing.
- Lieutenant John Gould Nicolas, R.N.
  In command of H.M.S. "Chelmer". Was twice wounded during the landing operations of 6th and 7th August, but refused to give up his duty of directing gunfire until no longer able to stand.
- Lieutenant Leonard George Addington, R.N.
  In command of H.M.S. "Usk" on 4th May 1915, at Gaba Tepe. Volunteered twice to go in to bring off wounded men, the beach and boat being at the time exposed to rifle and machine gun fire at close range.
- Flight Commander Charles Henry Butler, R.N.A.S.
- Flight Lieutenant Gordon Lindsay Thomson, R.N.A.S.
  These two pilots have carried out photographic work on many occasions flying at low altitudes over the enemy's lines to get good results.
- Flight Lieutenant Edwin Harris Dunning, R.N.A.S.
  Has performed exceptionally good work as a seaplane flyer, making many long flights both for spotting and photographing.
- Engineer Lieutenant Norman Seaton, R.N.
  Was in charge of the machinery of the motor-lighters. Displayed most untiring energy and zeal in this extremely important service, often under fire.
- Lieutenant Ernest Edward Madge, R.N.R.
  Performed good service during the landing on 25th April, under heavy fire, and on subsequent days.
- Lieutenant L. H. Strain, R.N.V.R.
  Has performed consistent good work as observer since February 1915.
- Lieutenant William Park, R.N.V.R.
  Has proved one of the most valuable spotting Officers and has frequently performed most useful service.

- Lieutenant Francis Hastings Thomas, R.M.L.I., H.M.S. "Talbot".
  Has on many occasions performed good service in keeping close touch from the shore between the military and his ship whilst the latter was supporting the Army.
- Acting Lieutenant David Laidlaw Cowan, R.N.R.
  Was in charge of a Whaler on the 6th June at Porta Jano, and rescued crew of H.M.S. "Euryalus's" picket boat under heavy fire.
- Acting Sub-Lieutenant John Edmund Sissmore R.N.
- Acting Sub-Lieutenant John Dyson Chapple, R.N.
- Midshipman Erskine Knollys Heveningham St. Aubyn, R.N.
  Have been continuously employed as observation Officers in aircraft since April and performed most valuable services.
- Midshipman Haydon Marriott Sutherland Forbes, R.N.
- Midshipman Maurice Charles Humphrey Lloyd, R.N.
  While under heavy fire on the 25th April, assisted to secure the lighters which formed a pier between the River Clyde and the shore.
- Midshipman William Henry Monier-Williams, R.N.
  On 25th April, though seriously wounded, brought his boat off the beach under fire, becoming unconscious after getting his boat clear.
- Midshipman Eric Wheler Bush, R.N.
- Midshipman Charles Douglas Horsfall Herbert Dixon, R.N.
- Midshipman Frederick Ernest Garner, R.N.
- Midshipman Raymond de Dibon Richardson, R.N.
- Probationery Midshipman Reginald Allen, R.N.R.
  All recommended for services performed under shell fire on the beaches and in steamboats off the beaches.
- Midshipman Henry Dunsmore Johnston, R.N.
  Assistant to Commander Swabey, Naval Observation Officer, Cape Helles, since July, 1915. Has shown great ability and resource to his most important duties.
- Gunner James Holden, R.N.
  Performed good service on "W" Beach, and always set a fine example.
- Signal Boatswain William James Scutt, R.N.
  In charge of Signal Station at Anzac since the 25th April.
- Acting Warrant Telegraphist John A. Britten, R.N.

Displayed great ability and resource in erecting Wireless Station at Cape Helles under fire. Served continuously there since 25th April.
- Skipper Frederick William Barnes, R.N.R.
  While off Anzac gallantly took in tow a tug under heavy fire.
- Skipper Robert W. Butler, R.N.R.
- Skipper George Mellership, R.N.R.
- Skipper Donald McBain Craig, R.N.R.
  In command of trawlers. Have performed long, arduous, and dangerous duties, and are specially selected from over a hundred names.

The KING has been graciously pleased to give orders for the award of the Distinguished Service Cross to the undermentioned Officers:—
LG 14.3.1916 p 2872

- Lieutenant Lionel Stanley Ormsby-Johnson, R.N.
  Flag Lieutenant to Vice-Admiral de Robeck. Did very good work in connection with Signal arrangements for the evacuation of Anzac and Suvla.
- Lieutenant Herbert Julian Carnduff, R.N.
  Did good service during the evacuation of Suvla and Helles, being specially selected for the latter.

The KING has been graciously pleased to give orders for the following awards of the Distinguished Service Cross to the under-mentioned Officers, in recognition of their services in the Patrol Cruisers, under the command of Rear-Admiral Sir Dudley R. S. De Chair, KCB, MVO, during the period ending the 31st December 1915:—
LG 31.3.1916 p 3516

- Lieutenant Marshal Llewelyn Clarke, R.N.
- Acting Lieutenant Percy Palfrey Crawford, R.N.R.
- Probationary Midshipman Cyril Assafrey Bamford, R.N.R.

The KING has been graciously pleased to approve of the award of the Distinguished Service Cross to Acting Lieutenant William Beswick, R.N.R.
LG 25.4.1916 p 4192

- A. Lieutenant William Beswick, R.N.R.

The KING has been graciously pleased to approve of the award of the Distinguished Service Cross to Eng. Lieutenant Leonard S. Loveless, R.N.R.
LG 28.4.1916 p 4264

- Eng. Lieutenant Leonard S. Loveless, R.N.R.

The KING has been graciously pleased to approve of the award of the Distinguished Service Cross to the undermentioned Officers in recognition of their services whilst employed on Transport duties at the Dardanelles:—
LG 31.5.1916 pp 5415/6

- Lieutenant Matthew Boggan, R.N.R., Troop Carrier "Ermine".
  Has carried out the arduous duties of ferry service between Mudros and the peninsula, carrying troops and military stores, entailing constant moving and going alongside other ships, in a zealous and most satisfactory manner, the service being frequently carried out under fire.
- Lieutenant Edward Davey, R.N.R., Cargo Carrier "Wheatberry".
  Whilst unloading alongside under the lee of the outer hulk, Helles beach, during a gale on 17th November 1915, the wind rose so suddenly that it was not considered safe for the ship to leave, and he was ordered to secure with extra hawsers. At the height of the gale one of the sternfasts parted, and it became evident that the ship would break adrift. Lieutenant Davey, with great judgement, eased off his lines, turned his ship in a very confined space, and successfully got her to sea.
- Lieutenant Archibald Lamont, R.N.R., Cargo Carrier "Asteria".
  In command of "Asteria", has done excellent work in carrying supplies to Cape Helles and other beaches. Always anxious to load quickly and proceed as often as possible, regardless of weather.
  Has frequently experienced heavy shell fire alongside the pier at Cape Helles during which he has coolly superintended the unloading of his ship.
- Acting Lieutenant Percival John Pycraft, R.N.R., H.M.S. "Europa".
  Whilst in command of a motor lighter this officer handled his craft in a most seamanlike manner, and on many occasions unloaded troops in bad weather, under the enemy's fire at Anzac, showing skill and ability.
- Sub-Lieutenant John Stewart, R.N.R., HM Tug "Flying Witch".

When HM Transport "East Point" containing hay and forage caught fire at Suvla, due to shell fire, this officer volunteered and offered his help; he worked for three hours under very trying conditions, and thereby greatly assisted in getting the fire under control.
- Midshipman George Tombeur Creft, R.N.R., H.M.S. "Europa".
  In command of a motor lighter. Has done excellent work off the Gallipoli Peninsula, landing troops and stores, often under shell fire, and especially during the evacuation of Cape Helles, when he handled his craft extremely well.
- Charles B. Andersson, Captain of H.M.T. "Roman Prince".
  Has carried out many trips between Mudros and the peninsula with valuable cargoes, the ship being generally used for conveyance of special material, such as guns, etc. Owing to this officer's zeal and energy the work has been carried out with invariable success. His ship has frequently been under fire, and he is a thorough seaman and handles his ship admirably.
- David P. McDonald, Captain of H.M.T. "Queen Louise".
  Has displayed great energy, determination and keenness in the working of his ship and for the special purposes for which she has been used, viz. taking guns and valuable cargo to the peninsula. His ship has been frequently under fire.
- Frederick Uren, Captain of H.M.T. "Trewellard". Has been frequently under fire off the peninsula. Has displayed much energy, determination and good seamanship.
- Lawrence V. James, Captain of H.M.T. "Huntsgreen".
  Took the place of H.M.S. "Hannibal" for the evacuation of Helles, and showed courageous and skilful handling of his ship.
- Robert Cumming, Captain of H.M.T. "Ajax". Performed good work off the eninsula where his ship was twice damaged by shell fire. Was attacked by enemy submarine on voyage from Alexandria to Mudros on 10th October 1915, and brought his ship safely into port.
- Harold J. Young, Captain of H.M.T. "East Point".
  Performed good work off the eninsula where his ship was set on fire by enemy shell fire, whilst unloading supplies.
- Alfred R. Murley, Chief Officer of H.M.T. "Cardiganshire".
  Responded to the call for volunteers to man S.S. "Jessie" on 22nd April 1915 and for a few

weeks during the first landing operations did invaluable work in keeping up an unfailing supply of ammunition to the beach.

- Harold G. E. Wightman, Officer Commanding cable ship "Levant".
Rendered good services in connection with the laying of the cable from Imbros to Suvla on the night of the Suvla landing, and in laying and repairing cables off the peninsula frequently under heavy fire.

The KING has been graciously pleased to approve of the award of the Distinguished Service Cross to the undermentioned Officers:—
LG 31.5.1916 p 5418

- Lieutenant George Arthur Coxall Sharpe, R.N.
In recognition of his services in a British submarine operating in the Baltic Sea.
- Lieutenant Alfred Edward Wainwright, R.N.V.R.
In recognition of his services in command of a motor boat on Lake Tanganyika on the occasion of the destruction of the German gunboat "Hedwig von Wissmann" on the 9th February 1916.
- Acting Lieutenant Joseph McLoughlin, R.N.R.
- Flight Sub-Lieutenant Henry Karslake Thorold, R.N.A.S.
- Sub-Lieutenant Reginald Henry Portal, R.N.
For conspicuous gallantry during a combat with an enemy aeroplane in the Dardanelles. At the outset Flight Sub-Lieutenant Thorold, the Pilot, was severely wounded in the back and Sub-Lieutenant Portal, the Observer, in the thigh and arm. The Pilot momentarily lost control and the machine nose dived, but he soon regained control and the Observer succeeded in firing another two magazines, whereupon the enemy aeroplane sheered off and disappeared. The Pilot took his machine safely back to the aerodrome, a distance of about twenty five miles, and after making a perfect landing, lost consciousness.
- Skipper Walter Samuel Wharton, R.N.R.
- Skipper Alfred Robert Thompson, R.N.R.

The KING has been graciously pleased to approve of the award of the Dinstinguished Service Cross to the undermentioned Officers:—
LG 22.6.1916 pp 6212/3

- Lieutenant Frank George Fowle, R.N.
In recognition of his services on the 18th January 1916, when he landed in charge of a demolition party from one of HM ships and blew up a railway bridge near Porto Lagos.

- Lieutenant Quentin Hunter Paterson, R.N.
- Lieutenant Alexander Boyd Greig, R.N.
In recognition of his services in one of HM submarines operating in the Baltic Sea.
- Flight Commander (Acting Squadron Commander) Francis Knox Haskins, R.N.
In recognition of his services as a pilot at Dunkirk since February 1915. He has taken part in air raids on Ostend and Zeebrugge, and has been continually employed in coastal reconnaissance.
- Lieutenant Douglas Claude Strathern Evill, R.N., Flight Commander, R.N.A.S.
In recognition of his services as a pilot at Dunkirk since February 1915. In addition to his work as a pilot, Flight Commander Evill has shown great zeal and ability in carrying out experiments connected with signalling and spotting.
- Lieutenant Desmond Neville Cooper Tufnell, R.N.
Lieutenant Tufnell has commanded a naval gun in an advanced position in Flanders since September 1915, and has frequently kept the gun in action under heavy and well directed fire. He has been mainly responsible for the mounting of some of the naval guns, in which he has shown great technical skill and energy.
- Flight Lieutenant John Joseph Petre, R.N.A.S.
In recognition of his services as a pilot at Dunkirk since February 1915. He has taken part in air raids on Ostend and Zeebrugge, during one of which he successfully engaged a hostile aeroplane of the Fokker type, and has carried out many coastal reconnaissances under shell fire.
- Flight Lieutenant Vincent Nicholl, R.N.A.S.
- Flight Lieutenant Frederick George Darby Hards, R.N.A.S.
In recognition of their services on the morning of the 25th April 1916 when they pursued a Zeppelin 65 miles out to sea, dived to within a few hundred feet of it, and attacked it with bombs and darts.
- Flight Lieutenant Charles Henry Chichester Smith, R.N.A.S.
In recognition of his services on the morning of the 25th April 1916 when he pursued a Zeppelin 50 miles out to sea, and on his return journey sighted the enemy fleet accompanied by submarines, which latter he attacked and compelled to submerge.
- Flight Lieutenant (Acting Flight Commander) George Henry Beard, R.N.A.S.
In recognition of his services as a pilot at Dunkirk since May 1915. He has carried out frequent reconnnaissances of the coast and has

continually been employed in aircraft and submarine patrols. He has twice attacked German submarines.

- Lieutenant Walter Larmond Scott, R.N.R.
- Flight Sub-Lieutenant Herbert Glynn Hall, R.N.A.S.

In recognition of his services on the morning of the 25th April 1916, when he carried out an air patrol with an observer during the attack by a raiding squadron of enemy ships on Yarmouth. Although severely wounded in the shoulder by shrapnel and weak from loss of blood, Flight Sub-Lieutenant Hall succeeded in piloting the machine back to his station and landed safely.

- Acting Lieutenant John Howell-Price, R.N.R.

In recognition of his services on the 29th February 1916, during the action between H.M.S. Alcantara and S.M.S. Greif.

- Lieutenant Charles William Nutting, R.N.V.R.
- Lieutenant Edward Raymond Peal, R.N.V.R.
- Sub Lieutenant Horace William Furnival, R.N.R.

In recognition of their services as aeroplane observers and continuous good work whilst attached to a Wing of the Royal Naval Air Service at Dunkirk.

- Engineer Sub-Lieutenant James William Grant, R.N.R.
- Temporary Lieutenant Gerald Fenwick Haszard, R.M.

In recognition of his services with the Royal Marine Artillery Anti-Aircraft Brigade in France. Lieutenant Haszard has on many occasions shown great coolness and resource under heavy fire, and has for several months, controlled his section in an advanced position with marked ability.

- Chief Carpenter Thomas Francis Barry, R.N.
- Carpenter Francis Rundell Hill, R.N.

In recognition of their services during the action between our cruisers and the enemy squadron which bombarded Lowestoft on the 25th April 1916.

- Skipper Thomas Charles Wylie, R.N.R.

The Lords Commissioners of the Admiralty have received with much satisfaction from the officers in charge of the Auxiliary Patrol areas at home and abroad reports on the services performed by the officers and men serving under their orders during the period 1st January 1915 to 31st January 1916. These reports show that the officers and men serving on Armed Yachts, Trawlers and Drifters of the Auxiliary Patrol during the period in question have carried out their duties under extremely arduous and hazardous conditions of weather

and exposure to enemy attack and mines with marked zeal, gallantry and success.

The KING has been graciously pleased to give orders for the following for the award of the Distinguished Service Cross to the under-mentioned officers in recognition of the services referred to in the reports mentioned above:—
LG 14.7.1916 pp 7065/6

- Lieutenant George Metcalfe Mercer, R.N.R.
- Lieutenant Albert James Coles, R.N.R.
- Lieutenant Horace Bowyer Smith, R.N.R.
- Lieutenant Vernon Lamonnarie Delves Broughton, R.N.R.
- Lieutenant George Worley, R.N.R.
- Lieutenant Henry James Bray, R.N.R.
- Lieutenant Hugh Holmes, R.N.R.
- Lieutenant Frederick Henry Peterson, R.N.R.
- Lieutenant William Rodger Mackintosh, R.N.R.
- Lieutenant Albert Charles Allman, R.N.R.
- Lieutenant Allan Lansley, R.N.R.
- Sub Lieutenant (now Act. Lieut-Cdr) Wybrants Olphert, R.N.R.
- Acting Lieutenant Walter George Morgan, R.N.R.
- Acting Lieutenant Robert Linaker, R.N.R.
- Sub-Lieutenant Thomas Francis Lanktree, R.N.R.
- Chief Gunner (now Lieutenant) Michael Carey, R.N.
- Skipper Jabez George King, R.N.R., 1436 W.S.A.
- Skipper Alexander Watt, R.N.R., 702 W.S.A.
- Skipper Albert Waters, R.N.R. 512 W.S.A.
- Skipper William Bruce, R.N.R. 1386 W.S.A.
- Skipper Andrew Noble Duthie, R.N.R. 1216 W.S.A.
- Skipper Leonard Morley, R.N.R. 414 SA
- Skipper Alfred Alexander, R.N.R. 152 W.S.A.
- Skipper James Edwin Mitchell Duncan, R.N.R. 1337 W.S.A.

The KING has been graciously pleased to give orders for the award of the Distinguished Service Cross to the undermentioned officers in recognition of their services in connection with the evacuation of the Serbian Army and Italian troops from Darazzo in December 1915, and January and February 1916:—
LG 14.7.1916 p 7067

- Acting Lieutenant Arnaud Adams, R.N.R.
- Acting Lieutenant Edward Maitland Rae, R.N.R.
- Acting Lieutenant Harry Cuthbertson Campbell Fry, R.N.R.
- Skipper Robert Aaron George, R.N.R. W.S.A.
- Skipper John Hughes, R.N.R. 1138 W.S.A.

- Skipper Frederick James Andrews, R.N.R. 937 W.S.A.
- Skipper William James Dow, R.N.R. 1257 W.S.A.
- Skipper William Cowie, R.N.R. 1488 W.S.A.
- Skipper Walter Charles Alfred Scrivener, R.N.R. 1924 W.S.A.
- Skipper Hugh Mortimer Nesling, R.N.R. 2107 W.S.A.

The KING has been graciously pleased to approve of the award of the Distinguished Service Cross to the undermentioned officers in recognition of the services stated:—
LG 14.7.1916 pp 7067/8

- Lieutenant Howard Canute Davis, R.D., R.N.R.
Lieutenant Davis was in command of the whaler which led the way into Tanga Harbour on the 19th August 1915.
- Lieutenant Herbert Keer Case, R.N.R.
Lieutenant Case was in command of one of the whalers which proceeded into Sudi Harbour on the 11th April 1916 and handled his vessel under fire in the confined waters of the harbour with great skill and gallantry. His quiet and calm behaviour set a perfect example to those under him.
- Boatswain John Park Mortimore, R.N.
Mr. Mortimore was in one of the whalers which entered Sudi Harbour on the 11th April 1916, and gave every assistance to his Captain, encouraging the guns' crews, making good spotting corrections, and rendering first aid readily and efficiently to the wounded.

The KING has been graciously pleased to give orders for the award of the Distinguished Service Cross to the undermentioned Officers:—
LG 6.9.1916 p 8768

- Lieutenant Frederick Septimus Kelly, R.N.V.R.
- Captain Bernard George Weller, R.M.L.I.
- Temporary Lieutenant Thomas Nixon Riley, R.M.
In recognition of their services with the Royal Naval Division in the Gallipoli Peninsula.
- Flight Sub-Lieutenant Roderic Stanley Dallas, R.N.A.S.
Flight Sub-Lieutenant Dallas, in addition to performing consistently good work in reconnaissances and fighting patrols since December 1915, has been brought to notice by the Vice-Admiral, Dover Patrol, for the specially gallant manner in which he has carried out his duties. Amongst other exploits is the following: On the 21st May 1916, he sighted at least 12 hostile machines, which had been bombing Dunkerque. He attacked one at 7,000 feet, and then attacked a second machine close to him. After re-loading, he climbed to 10,000 feet, and attacked a large hostile two seater machine off Westende. The machine took fire and nose dived seawards. Another enemy machine then appeared, which he engaged and chased to the shore, but had to abandon owing to having used all his ammunition.

- Sub-Lieutenant (now Acting Lieutenant) Christopher Bernard Oxley, R.N.
Sub-Lieutenant Oxley was acting as Observer with Flight Lieutenant Edward H. Dunning, DSC, as Pilot, on escort and reconnaissance patrol for a flight of bombing machines on the Bulgarian coast, on the 20th June, 1916. Two enemy machines were engaged at close range and forced to retire, and as our machine withdrew Flight Lieutenant Dunning was hit in the left leg and the machine itself was badly damaged. Sub Lieutenant Oxley, having first improvised a tourniquet, which he gave to Flight Lieutenant Dunning, took control of the machine, whilst the latter put on the tourniquet. The pilot was obliged to keep his thumb over a hole in the lower part of the petrol tank in order to keep enough fuel to return to the aerodrome, where he made an exceedingly good landing.
- Flight Sub Lieutenant Donald Ernest Harkness, R.N.A.S.
- Flight Sub Lieutenant Ralph Harold Collett, R.N.A.S.
In recognition of their services on the morning of the 9th August 1916, when they dropped bombs on the airship sheds at Evere and Berchem St. Agathe. Flight Sub Lieutenant Collett dropped all his bombs on the shed at Evere from a height of between 300 and 500 feet, under a very heavy rifle, machine gun and shrapnel fire from all directions. Flight Sub Lieutenant Harkness could not descend so low owing to the very heavy anti aircraft fire which had by this time been opened on the machines, but he dropped some of his bombs on the shed, and then proceeded to Berchem St. Agathe, which he also bombed.
- Acting Lieutenant Frank Stewart Lofthouse, R.N.R.
Lieutenant Lofthouse showed admirable presence of mind on the occasion of the attack by an Austrian cruiser on a group of drifters in the Adriatic on the 9th July 1916. When the cruiser opened fire on his drifter at point blank range, this officer ordered the crew to put on lifebelts, and immediately went to the wireless

apparatus himself and twice sent out a message as to the presence of the cruiser. Whilst he was sending the message three shots hit the ship. He then came on deck and finding his ship was sinking, he got his crew overboard and by his example and behaviour kept them together until they were picked up six hours later.

- Skipper Harold John Goldspink, R.N.R. 1937, W.S.A.
- Skipper James Ritchie, R.N.R. 1271, W.S.A.
  Skipper Ritchie behaved in an admirable manner and displayed great coolness under fire on the occasion of the attack by an Austrian cruiser on a group of drifters in the Adriatic on the 9th July 1916. He was instrumental in saving many lives by taking his drifter alongside damaged drifters and by picking up men who were in the water.
- Skipper Frederick George Harris, R.N.R., 1147 W.S.A.
  Skipper Harris showed most seamanlike qualities on the occasion of the attack by an Austrian cruiser on a group of drifters in the Adriatic on the 9th July 1916. He went to the assistance of the damaged drifters, took them in tow and brought them safely into harbour.

The KING has been graciously pleased to give orders for the award of the Distinguished Service Cross to the undermentioned Officers in recognition of their services as mentioned in the foregoing despatch (Battle of Jutland 31st May to the 1st June 1916, *LG 6.7.1916 pp 6713/26*):—
LG 15.9.1916 p 9071

- Lieutenant Arthur Malcolm Peters, RN
- Lieutenant Cuthbert Coppinger, RN
- Lieutenant John Hinton Carrow, RN
- Lieutenant Stewart Magee Walker, RN
- Flight Lieutenant Frederick Joseph Rutland, RN (Lieutenant RN)
  Extract from Despatch.
  From a report from Galateu at 2.25pm it was evident that the enemy force was considerable, and not merely an isolate unit of light cruisers, so at 2.45pm I ordered "Engadine" (Lieutenant Commander C. G. Robinson) to send up a seaplane and scout to NNE. This order was carried out very quickly, and by 3.8pm a seaplane, with Flight Lieutenant F. J. Rutland, RN, as pilot, and Assistant Paymaster G. S. Trewin, RN, as observer, was well under way; her first reports of the enemy were received in Engadine about 3.30pm. Owing to clouds it was necessary to fly very low, and in order to identify four enemy light cruisers the seaplane had to fly at a height of 900 feet within 3,000

yards of them, the light cruisers opening fire on her with every gun that would bear. This in no way interfered with the clarity of their reports, and both Flight Lieutenant Rutland and Assistant Paymaster Trewin are to be congratuled on their achievement, which indicates that seaplanes under such circumstances are of distinct value.

- Lieutenant John Gordon Cliff-McCulloch, RNR
- Lieutenant Percy Harrison, RNVR
- Carpenter Lieutenant John Norman Matheson, RN
- The Reverend Anthony Pollen (Roman Catholic Chaplain)
- Sub Lieutenant Newton James Wallop William-Powlett, RN
- Surgeon Probationer Douglas George Patrick Bell, RNVR
- Chief Artificer Engineer Alexander Noble, RN
- Artificer Engineer Joseph House, RN

The KING has been graciously pleased to approve of the award of the Distinguished Service Cross to the undermentioned Officers:—
LG 25.10.1916 p 10362

- Lieutenant Stephen Clive Lyttelton, RN
- Lieutenant Rodolph Henry Fane De Salis, RN
- Lieutenant Anthony Bevis Lockhart, RN
  In recognition of his services in submarines in enemy waters.
- Lieutenant George Samuel Brown, RN
- Lieutenant James Lawrence Boyd, RN
- Lieutenant Douglas Carteret Sealy, RN
- Lieutenant Adrian Henry James Stokes, RN
  In recognition of their services in submarines in enemy waters.
- Flight Commander Tom Harry England, RNAS
  In recognition of his services on the 26th August 1916, when, accompanied by a Military Officer as Observer, he flew a seaplane 43 miles inland from the Syrian Coast, crossed a range of hills 2,000 feet high, with clouds at 1,500 feet, and after dropping bombs on the station of Homs returned safely to his ship. The machine was exposed to rifle fire at extremely low altitudes for long periods, and Flight Commander England showed remarkable pluck, determination and skill in carrying out the flight under adverse conditions.
- Flight Lieutenant Charles Teverill Freeman, RNAS.
  In recognition of the gallantry and skill displayed by him on the night of the 2nd August 1916, when he made a determined attack on a Zeppelin at sea, only abandoning the attack when he had exhausted all his

ammunition. As darkness was approaching at
the time, and his chances of being picked up
were problematical, his courage and devotion
in returning to the attack a second and third
time were exemplary.

- Flight Sub Lieutenant Stanley James Goble,
RNAS
In recognition of his services on the 24th
September 1916, when he attacked two hostile
machines in the vicinity of Ghistelles at close
range, and brought one of them down on fire
in a spiral nose dive.
- Flight Sub Lieutenant Ronald Grahame, RNAS
For exceptional gallantry in attacking and
beating off four enemy seaplanes whilst on
escort duty off the Belgian coast on the 22nd
September 1916.
- Flight Sub Lieutenant Daniel Murray Boyne
Galbraith, RNAS
In recognition of his services in attacking a
large enemy two seater seaplane on the 28th
September 1916. Flight Sub Lieutenant
Galbraith's machine was severely damaged by
gun fire from the enemy machine, which finally
blew up in the air.
- Sub Lieutenant (now Acting Lieutenant) John
Gwyndd Wood, RNR.
Sub Lieutenant Wood was sent down the river
Tigris from Umm-al-Tubal Camp in a motor
boat about 2.0am on the 1st December 1915,
with an important message. He displayed great
bravery under heavy fire and was wounded.
- Lieutenant Benjamin Rowley George Kent, RNR
- Acting Lieutenant Hugh Donald Wynne, RNR
- Sub-Lieutenant Frederick Henry Good, RNR
- Chief Gunner Robert John Thomas, RN
In recognition of their services in the Patrol
Cruisers during the period January to June
1916.
- Acting Lieutenant Denis A. Casey, RNR
- Acting Lieutenant Arthur George Madan, RNR
In recognition of their services in submarines in
enemy waters.
- Gunnery (T) Reuben James McVittie, RN
- Skipper Charles Angus, RNR 390 WSA
In recognition of his conduct in an engagement
with enemy submarines on the 11th July 1916,
and of the skilful and seamanlike manner in
which he manoeuvered his vessel when she
was disabled by gunfire, thereby saving
practically the whole of his ship's company.

The KING has been graciously pleased to
approve of the award of a Bar to the
Distinguished Service Cross of the undermentioned Warrant Officer for a subsequent act
of gallantry:—

LG 25.10.1916 p 10362

- Skipper Alfred Robert Thompson, DSC, RNR
(The award of the Distinguished Service Cross
was notified in *London Gazette* dated 31st May
1916, page 5418).
The KING has been graciously pleased to
approve of the award of the Distinguished
Service Cross to the undermentioned
Officers:—
LG 5.12.1916 p 11842

- Flight Lieutenant Egbert Cadbury, RNAS
- Flight Sub Lieutenant Gerrard William Reginald
Fane, RNAS
In recognition of the skill and gallantry, which
they displayed on the morning of the 28th
November 1916, in pursuing out to sea and
attacking at close range a Zeppelin, which had
been engaged in a raid on England. Both
officers were exposed to machine gun fire
throughout their attacks.

The KING has been graciously pleased to
approve the award of the Distinguished Service
Cross to the following officers of the British
Mercantile Marine in recognition of zeal and
devotion to duty shown in carrying on the
trade of the country during the war:—
LG 22.12.1916 p 12559

- Captain Charles John Walker
- Captain Henry Vaughan Rigby
- Captain James Trickey
- Captain Alban Chittenden
- Captain George Wallace Cockman, RD
(Commander RNR, retired)
- Captain Frederick Hubert Robinson
- Captain Frederick Edward Beeching
- Chief Officer Frank Aubrey McGowan
Richardson
- Captain James Ernest Churchill (Lieutenant RNR
retired)
- Captain Edward Borrowdale Johnson
- Captain George Richard Thompson

The KING has been graciously pleased to give
orders for the award of the Distinguished
Service Cross to the undermentioned Officers in
recognition of their services in the Battle of
Jutland.
LG 1.1.1917 p 7

- Mr. Francis William Potter, Gunner, RN
For very important duties during the action
carried out with great coolness and accuracy.
- Mr. Thomas Bazley, Gunner (T) RN
Was of great assistance during action on night
of 31st May – 1st June. In charge of torpedo

armament of ship, and fired at enemy's Battle Fleet during the night with effect.

The KING has been graciously pleased to give orders for the award of the Distinguished Service Cross to the undermentioned Officers in recognition of their bravery and devotion to duty during minesweeping operations:—
LG 1.1.1917 p 8

- Lieutenant Peter Alexander Crawford Sturrock, RN
- Lieutenant Arthur Edgar Buckland, RN
- Temporary Lieutenant James Collis Bird, RN (Lieutenant RIM retd)
- Lieutenant William G. Wood, RNR
- Lieutenant Geoffrey Unsworth, RNR
- Lieutenant Rudolph Lancelot Wikner, RNR
- Lieutenant William St. Clair Fleming, RNR
- Lieutenant John Percival Tugwood, RNR
- Acting Lieutenant William George Duggan, RNR
- Skipper Frederick Alfred Sibley, RNR 20 WSA
- Skipper Benjamin Robert Joyce, RNR 60 WSA
- Skipper George Ferguson, RNR 233 WSA
- Skipper Alexander McLeod, RNR 303 WSA
- Skipper Alexander McKay, RNR 356 WSA
- Skipper Donald McMillan RNR 2010 WSA
- Skipper Samson Herbert Hayes RNR 2118 WSA

The KING has been graciously pleased to give orders for the award of the Distinguished Cross to the undermentioned Officers in recognition of their services:—
LG 1.1.1917 pp 10/11

- Flight Lieut. Ernest William Norton, RNAS
  In recognition of his skill and gallantry in destroying a German kite balloon on the 20th October 1916 under severe anti-aircraft fire.
- Surgeon Hother McCormack Hanschell RN
  In recognition of his services with the Tanganyika Flotilla the comparative immunity from sickness enjoyed by the members of the expedition was due to the unremitting care bestowed by Hanschell on the health of the personnel and on the sanitary state of the camps and vessels
- Lieutenant Arthur Darville Dudley RNVR
  In recognition of his services with the Tanganyika Flotilla. He showed great coolness and skill in handling his ship in all circumstances
- Sub-Lieut. Guy Trevarton Sholl RNVR
  In recognition of his services in charge of a squadron of Royal Naval Armoured Cars in Armenia and Persia. By his presence of mind he saved the cars when they were ambushed by the Turks at Marnik on the 1st September

1916 and by his devotion to duty, courage and hard work he effected the capture of the village of Norschen on the 9th September, and secured the explosion of a Turkish magazine, with great loss to the enemy. His consistent cheerfulness and unselfishness were a material factor in the of work accomplished by the cars

- Gunner (T) James Albert Graham, RN
  In recognition of his services in a submarine, which carried out a successful attack on an enemy Battle Squadron on the 5th November 1916
- Captain John Couch, Master of the Transport "Trevorian"
  In recognition of the great coolness judgment and resource which he displayed under very trying circumstances during the evacuation on the 22nd October, 1916. The "Trevorian" was the last ship to leave the harbour, which was already being shelled, was exposed to shell fire for an hour after putting out to sea, and successfully avoided a submarine attack during the voyage. During the whole of this time Captain Couch remained on the bridge.

The KING has been graciously pleased to approve of the award of the Distinguished Service Cross to the following Officers:—
LG 16.2.1917 pp 1648/9

- Lieut John Lawrie RNR
- Lieut Cedric Naylor RNR
- Act Lieut Philip James Hogg RNR
- Ch Gnr (T) Richard Hawkes RN
- Flight Cdr William Geoffrey Moore RNAS
  In recognition of the excellent work which he has done in East Africa, and especially on the 10th January 1917, when he flew a distance of 300 miles from Ubena to Mahenje. He obtained important results in bombing flights
- Flight Lieut Lionel Conrad Shoppee RNAS
  For conspicuous gallantry and enterprise during a bomb attack by aircraft on an important enemy railway bridge. A subsequent reconnaissance showed that the whole of the centre section of the bridge had collapsed into the river, thereby interrupting important enemy railway communications
- Flight Lieut Edward Rochfort Grange RNAS
  For conspicuous gallantry and skill on several occasions in successfully attacking and bringing down hostile machines, particularly on the 4th January 1917, when during one flight he had three separate engagements with hostile machines, all of which were driven down out of control. On the 5th January, 1917, he attacked three hostile machines, one of which was driven down in a nose dive. On the 7th

January, 1917, after having driven down one hostile machine, he observed two other enemy aircraft attacking more of our scouts. He was on the way to give assistance when he was attacked by a third hostile scout. He was hit in the shoulder by a bullet from this machine, but landed his aeroplane in an aerodrome on our side of the lines.

● Flight Sub-Lieut Robert Alexander Little, RNAS
For conspicuous bravery in successfully attacking and bringing down hostile machines on several occasions On 11th November 1916, he attacked and brought down a hostile machine in flames. On 12th November 1916 he attacked a German machine at a range of 50 yards, this machine was brought down in a nose- dive On 20th November 1916, he dived at a hostile machine, and opened fire at 25 yards range, the observer was seen to fall down inside the machine, which went down in a spinning nose dive. On 1st January, 1917, he attacked an enemy scout, which turned over on its back and came down completely out of control.

The KING has been graciously pleased to approve of the award to the undermentioned Officer of a Bar to his Distinguished Service Cross:—
LG 16.2.1917 p 1649

● Flight Lieut Daniel Murray Boyne Galbraith, DSC RNAS
For conspicuous gallantry. On 23rd November 1916, he attacked single-handed a formation of six hostile aircraft, no other allied machines being in the vicinity. One hostile machine was shot down, a second was driven down under control, and the remaining four machines then gave up the fight and landed. In several other combats in the air Flight Lieutenant Galbraith has displayed exceptional gallantry, particularly on 10th and 16th November 1916, on each of which days he successfully engaged and shot down an enemy machine.
(The award of the Distinguished Service Cross was announced in the *London Gazette* of the 25th October 1916.)

The KING has been graciously pleased to approve of the award of the Distinguished Service Cross to the undermentioned officers:—
LG 23.3.1917 p 2951/2

● Capt John Maurice Palmer RMLI
● Lieut Edward Overend Priestley RN
● Lieut Arthur Francis Eric Palliser RN
● Lieut Leon Stopford Acheson RNR

● Lieut William Arthur Hanna RNR
● Act Lieut Francis Cecil Pretty RNR
● Act Lieut James Sinclair Campbell RNR
● Act Lieut Edgar William Bowack RNR
● Act Lieut Stephen Philip Robey White RNR
● Act Lieut Magnus Leo Musson RNR
● Act Lieut Francis Robert Hereford RNR
● Asst Payr William Richard Ashton RNR
● Sub-Lieut Leonard Clifton Warder RNR
● Sub-Lieut Richard Percy Nisbet RNR
● Asst Payr Reginald Arthur Nunn RNR
● Gnr (T) Harry Morgan RN
● Gnr Morris Roseman Cole RN
● Skipper George Albert Novo RNR 1338 WSA
● Skipper David Wallace RNR 1443 WSA
● Skipper Philip William Page RNR 559 WSA
● Skipper Thomas Crisp RNR 10055 DA

The KING has been graciously pleased to approve of the award to the undermentioned Officer of a Bar to the Distinguished Service Cross for a subsequent act of gallantry
LG 23.3.1917 p 2952

● Skipper Walter Samuel Wharton DSC RNR
(The award of the Distinguished Service Cross was announced in *London Gazette* dated 31st May 1916.)

In addition to the honours notified in the Supplements to the *London Gazette* dated 14th March, 15th May (3rd Supplement) and 31st May 1916 (3rd Supplement)

The KING has been graciously pleased to give orders for the award of the Distinguished Service Cross to the undermentioned officers, in recognition of their services in the Eastern Mediterranean up to the 30th June 1916:—
LG 11.4.1917 pp 3477/8

● Lieutenant Kenneth Edwards RN
Performed good service at the landing and at the evacuation of Helles. Set a fine example to his men whilst assisting at salvage operations on Monitor M. 30 under fire from enemy's guns.
● Lieutenant Charles Leonard Fawell, RNVR
For consistent good service, often under heavy fire, whilst in command of motor gun-boat in the Smyrna inner patrol

The KING has been graciously pleased to give orders for the award of the Distinguished Service Cross to the undermentioned Officers in recognition of their services in the Patrol Cruisers, under the command of Vice-Admiral Reginald G. O. Tupper, C.B., C.V.O. during the period 1st July – 31st December, 1916

LG 21.4.1917 p 3819

- Asst Payr (now Payr) Frank Lankester Horsey, RN
- Lieut Howard Uncles RNR
- Mid. Thomas Edwin Hunter Grove, RNR

The KING has been graciously pleased to approve of the award of the Distinguished Service Cross to the undermentioned Officers:—
LG 21.4.1917 p 3820

- Flt. Lieut. (now act. Flt-Cdr) Charles Cyril Rogers Edwards, RNAS
- Sub. Lieut. Charles Keith Chase, RNVR
In recognition of their services on the 1st March 1917, when they were attacked by two hostile machines whilst on a reconnaissance flight and brought them both down out of control. Flight Lieut. Edwards was hit by a bullet which passed through the left shoulder, fracturing the collar bone, and at the same time was slightly wounded in both feet. Although suffering considerably, he brought his machine home safely, in spite of being again attacked by two hostile aircraft. By his determination and pluck he probably saved his own life and that of his observer.
- Flt. Cdr. Alfred William Clemson, RNAS
- Sub-Lieut. James Leslie Kerry, RNVR
In recognition of their conspicuous gallantry on the 28th February 1917, when they carried out a reconnaissance of Rayak and Damascus in a seaplane. During this flight they crossed two mountain ranges whose lowest ridges are 4,000 feet high, and brought back valuable information.
- Lieut. (now Lieut. Cdr) Erskine Childers, RNVR
In recognition of his services with the RNAS for the period January-May, 1916. During this time he acted as observer in many important air reconnaissances, showing remarkable aptitude for observing and for collating the results of his observation.
- Sub-Lieut. Horace Ernest Philip Wigglesworth RNAS
For conspicuous gallantry and enterprise on the 23rd January, 1917, during a bomb attack by aircraft when considerable damage was done to enemy blast furnaces at Burbach. During this flight he fought five engagements with enemy aircraft in formations of three, four and five at a time.
- Sub-Lieut. (now Lieut) Eric Bourne Coulter Betts, RNVR
In recognition of his services on the 1st February, 1917, when he carried out a long reconnaissance and returned with extremely important information, shooting down an enemy scout machine which attacked him on his way back.

The KING has been graciously pleased to approve of the award of the Distinguished Service Cross to the undermentioned Officers:—
LG 21.4.1917 pp 3820/1

- Act. Lieut. John Herman Ritchie Elfert, RNR.
- Eng. Sub-Lieut. John Smith, RNR
- Gnr. William John Hubbard, RN
- Art. Eng. Ernest Thaxter, RN
Honours for Service in the Action between HM Ships Swift and Broke and German Destroyers on the night of the 20th to 21st April 1917.

The KING has been graciously pleased to give orders for the award of the Distinguished Service Cross to the undermentioned Officers for their services during this action.
LG 10.5.1917 pp 4181/2

- Lieut. Geoffrey Victor Hickman, RN.
Navigator and second in command of HMS "Broke". He assisted with great coolness in handling the ship in action. His proper appreciation of the situation when one enemy destroyer was torpedoed, which his commanding officer had made ready to ram, enabled course to be altered in time to ram the next astern.
- Lieut. Robert Douglas King-Harman, RN
Navigating Officer of HMS "Swift". He was of the utmost assistance to his commanding officer throughout.
- Lieut. Maximilian Carden Despard, RN.
First and Gunnery Lieut. of HMS "Broke". He controlled gun fire and gave the orders which resulted in an enemy destroyer being torpedoed.
- Lieut. Henry Antony Simpson, RN.
Executive Officer and Gunnery Lieut. of HMS "Swift". He displayed great coolness and method in the control of fire which he had very ably organised and zealously drilled, and greatly assisted his commanding officer throughout the action.
- Surg. Prob. Christopher Thomas Helsham, RNVR. ("Broke").
- Surg. Prob. John Sinclair Westwater, RNVR. ("Swift")
Worked with great energy and ability in attending to the wounded.
- Gnr. (T) Henry Turner, RN ("Swift").

Obtained a hit with a torpedo on one of the enemy destroyers.

- Gnr. (T) Frederick Grinney, RN. ("Broke")
  Gave orders for the firing of the torpedo which struck one of the enemy destroyers.
- Mid. Donald Allen Gyles, RNR. ("Broke")
  He took charge on the forecastle and although wounded in the eye, organised a gun's crew from the survivors of the crews which had suffered heavy casualties and kept the guns on the forecastle going. He repelled the German sailors who swarmed on board from the destroyer which was rammed, and remained at his post until after the action was finished.

The KING has been graciously pleased to approve of the award of the Distinguished Service Cross to the undermentioned Officers:—
LG 12.5.1917 pp 4625/6.

- Flt. Cdr. Bertram Lawrence Huskisson, RNAS.
  For conspicuous skill and gallantry during the past eighteen months. This officer led his flight with great courage and determination during the three months he was attached to the Royal Flying Corps, and has destroyed or driven down several hostile machines.
- Flt. Lieut. (now Flt. Cdr) Arthur Dennis Wigram Allen, RNAS.
  This officer has done a very large amount of flying during the past nine months on fast scouts on fighter patrol work. In addition, he has done a great deal of testing work at the aircraft depot. He is a brilliant pilot.
- Flt. Lieut (Now Flt. Cdr) Bertram Charles Bell, DSO, RNAS.
  For conspicuous skill and gallantry during the last fifteen months. This officer has had charge of a flight during this period, and has continuously carried out most valuable work as a pilot both of reconnaissance and photographic and of fighter escort machines. His machine has been constantly under heavy anti aircraft fire for long periods while carrying out his work.
- Flt. Lieut. (now actg. Flt Cdr) Frank Fowler, RNAS.
  For conspicuous skill and gallantry during the last nine months in reconnaissance, photographic and spotting machines. On the majority of occasions he has acted as pilot to Lieut. Gow, RNVR, his machine being constantly hit by anti aircraft fire.
- Flt. Lieut. Frank Thomas Digby, RNAS.
  For conspicuously good work as a pilot of bombing machines. He has taken part in numerous bomb raids with successful results.

- Flt. Lieut. Herbert George Brackley, RNAS.
  For conspicuously good work as pilot of a bombing machine. Has carried out twelve raids since the 1st June 1916, mostly by night. On one occasion he returned with forty holes in his machine.
- Flt. Lieut. Noel Keeble, RNAS.
  For conspicuous gallantry on the 23rd October 1916, when he attacked four German seaplanes and brought one of them down in a vertical nose dive into the sea.
- Flt. Lieut. Thomas Frederick Le Mesurier, RNAS.
  For conspicuous work as a pilot of a bombing machine. Has taken part in fourteen raids and numerous fighter patrols.
- Flt. Lieut. Irwin Napier Colin Clarke, RNAS.
  For conspicuously good work as a pilot of bombing machines. He has taken part in seventeen attacks with good results, in addition to carrying out numerous fighter patrols.
- Flt. Lieut. Robert John Orton Compston, RNAS.
  For conspicuous skill and gallantry during the past nine months, in particular when attached to the Royal Flying Corps, when he had numerous engagements with enemy aircraft, and certainly destroyed one.
- Flt. Lieut. William Edward Gardner, RNAS.
  For conspicuously good work as a pilot of a bombing machine. He has taken part in seventeen raids and numerous fighter patrols.
- Lieut. Russell William Gow, RNVR.
  For consistently good work when acting as observer, being responsible for many valuable photographs; also for his good work in connection with artillery spotting. His machine has been hit on many occasions by anti aircraft fire.
- Flt. Sub Lieut. Philip Sidney Fisher, RNAS.
  For conspicuous skill as a seaplane pilot during the last nine months. Has carried out many valuable reconnaissance patrols and several bomb attacks with good results.
- Flt. Sub. Lieut. Douglas Alexander Hardy Nelles, RNAS.
  For conspicuously good work as a pilot of a bombing machine. He has taken part in seventeen raids and has also done a large amount of fighter patrol work.
- Flt. Sub. Lieut. Ernest John Cuckney, RNAS.
  For conspicuous gallantry and ability when taking part in a raid on the seaplane station at Zeebrugge.

- Flt. Sub. Lieut. John Edward Sharman, RNAS.
  For devotion to duty during long distance air raids. On one occasion, after leading a flight in the morning and returning safely he volunteered and flew a bombing machine with a second flight in the afternoon, again acting as leader.
- Flt. Sub. Lieut. Walter Ernest Flett, RNAS.
  For conspicuous gallantry during an air raid. Shortly after leaving the objective he was engaged with three enemy machines, two single seater and one two seater. His gunlayer, Air Mechanic, 1st Grade, R. G. Kimberley, was slightly wounded in the wrist, which numbed his hand. Notwithstanding this he succeeded in bringing down two of the enemy machines, being again wounded by an explosive bullet in the ankle. The machine was riddled with bullets, and owing to the damage navigation was most difficult, and the return journey was very slow. Consequently he was again attacked, but although the gunlayer was twice wounded, the enemy machine was driven off.

The KING has been graciously pleased to approve of the award to the undermentioned Officer of a Bar to the Distinguished Service Cross:—
LG 12.5.1917 p 4626

- Flt. Lieut. Ronald Grahame, DSC, RNAS.
  For conspicuous gallantry during raids on the seaplane station at Zeebrugge. On one occasion he descended to 600 feet, and on another occasion to 300 feet, before releasing his bombs.
  (The award of the Distinguished Service Cross was announced in *London Gazette* dated 25th October 1916).

The KING has been graciously pleased to approve of the award of the Distinguished Service Cross to the undermentioned Officers:—
LG 12.5.1917 p 4627.

- Lieut. Walter Napier Thomason Beckett, RN
- Engr. Lt. Alexander Hargreaves Boyle, RN
- Lieut. Frank Tomkinson Brade, RNR
- Lieut. Alfred Swann, RNVR
- Act. Lieut. James Alexander Pollard Blackburn, RNR
- Act. Lieut. William Murdoch McLeod, RNR
- Act. Lieut. Arnold George Morgan, RNR
- Act. Lieut. Harold William Green, RNR
- Asst. Payr. John Weston Sells, RNR
- Sub Lieut. Harold Drew, RN

- Act. Sub Lieut. (actg) Edmund George Smithard, RNR
- Ch. Art. Engr. Edward Ethelbert Rose, RN
- Gnr. Percy John Joseph Cullum, RN
- Skipper Joseph Powley, RNR, 240 SA.
- Skipper William Wood, RNR, 648 SA.
- Skipper James Thompson

The KING has been graciously pleased to approve of the award to the undermentioned Officer of a Bar to the Distinguished Service Cross for a subsequent act of gallantry:—
LG 12.5.1917 p 4627

- Lieut. Walter Larmond Scott, DSC, RNR (since drowned)
  (The award of the Distinguished Service Cross was announced in the *London Gazette* dated 22nd June 1916).

The KING has been graciously pleased to approve the award of the Distinguished Service Cross to the following officers of the British Mercantile Marine, in recognition of zeal and devotion to duty shown in carrying on the trade of the country during the war:—
LG 12.5.1917 p 4628

- Capt. Frederick John Lane
- Capt. John Harrie Howard Scudamore
- Ch. Off. James Black Ruhe
- Ch. Eng. Thomas Dix Lowthian
- 2nd Off. William Foster
- Ch. Eng. Alexander Graham Stewart
- Capt. Andrew McIntosh McKend
- Capt. Patterson Kirkaldy
- Ch. Off. Harry Rawcliffe
- Ch. Eng. Alexander Rose Arthur

The KING has been graciously pleased to give orders for the award of the Distinguished Service Cross to the undermentioned officers in recognition of their services in the Destroyer Patrol Flotillas, Armed Boarding Steamers, &c, during the period which ended on the 30th September 1916:—
LG 23.5.1917 pp 5049/50

- Lieut. (now Lieut. Cdr) Henry Radcliffe James, RN
- Lieut. Cecil Rudolph Ernest Wilbraham Perryman, RN
- Lieut. Keith Richard Farquharson, RN
- Lieut. Herbert Owen, RN
- Lieut. Ernest Kirkbank Irving, RNR
- Lieut. William Murray, RNR
- Act. Lieut. Thomas Henry Coughtry, RNR
- Act. Lieut. Albert Ernest Trivett Morris, RNR
- Asst. Payr. Hugh James Leleu, RNR

- Ch. Gnr. Reginald Cardwell, IDE
- Ch. Art. Engr. Herbert Edward Pope, RN
- Ch. Art. Engr. John William Farrow, RN
- Gnr Thomas Henry Keyes, RN
- Art. Engr. William Thomas Hall, RN.

To receive a Bar to the Distinguished Service Cross.
- Lieut. Henry Antony Simpson, DSC, RN.

The KING has been graciously pleased to approve the award of the Distinguished Service Cross to the undermentioned officers in recognition of their services in vessels of the Dover Patrol, under the command of Vice Admiral Sir Reginald H. S. Bacon, KCB, KCVO, DSO.
LG 23.5.1917 pp 5051/2

- Lieut. John Brooke, RN
- Lieut. Sir John Meynell Alleyne, Bart, RN.
- Lieut. Wyndham Charles Johnson, RN
- Lieut. Charles Herbert Lightoller, RNR
- Sub. Lieut. John Douglas Gibbon Chater, RNR
- Ch. Art. Eng. Henry Taylor, RN
- Gnr. George Gates, RN

The KING has been graciously pleased to approve of the award of the Distinguished Service Cross to the undermentioned officers:—
LG 23.5.1917 p 5053

- Lieut. Francis William Crowther, RN
- Lieut. William Strickland Harrison, RNR
- Act. Lieut. Charles Bruce Long Filmer, RNR
- Sub Lieut. Charles O'Callaghan, RN
- Sub. Lieut. Lawrence James Meade, RNR

The undermentioned officers have been awarded a Bar to the Distinguished Service Cross for subsequent acts of gallantry:—
- Lieut. Cedric Naylor, DSC, RNR.
(The award of the Distinguished Service Cross was announced in the *London Gazette* dated 16th February 1917).
- Act. Lieut. Stephen Philip Robey White, DSC, RNR
(The award of the Distinguished Service Cross was announced in the *London Gazette* dated 23rd March 1917).
- Asst. Payr. William Richard Ashton, DSC, RNR.
(The award of the Distinguished Service Cross was announced in the *London Gazette* dated 23rd March 1917).

The KING has been graciously pleased to approve of the award of the Distinguished Service Cross to the undermentioned Officers:—

LG 23.5.1917 p 5053/4

- Flt. Lieut. Lloyd Samuel Breadner, RNAS
For conspicuous gallantry and skill in leading his patrol against hostile formations. He has himself brought down three hostile machines and forced several others to land.
On the 6th April 1917, he drove down a hostile machine which was wrecked while attempting to land in a ploughed field.
On the morning of the 11th April 1917, he destroyed a hostile machine, which fell in flames, brought down another in a spinning nose dive with one wing folded up, and forced a third to land.
- Flt. Sub. Lieut. Joseph Stewart Fall, RNAS
For conspicuous bravery and skill in attacking hostile aircraft. On the morning of the 11th April 1917, while escorting our bombing machines, he brought down three hostile aircraft. The first he attacked and brought down completely out of control. He was then attacked by three hostile scouts who forced him down to within about two hundred feet of the ground. By skilful piloting he manoeuvred his machine close behind one of them, which was driven down and wrecked. Shortly afterwards this Officer was again attacked by a hostile scout, which he eventually brought down a short time before recrossing the lines. He then landed at one of the aerodromes, his machine having been riddled with bullets from the hostile machines, and also by rifle fire from the ground.

The KING has been graciously pleased to approve of the award of the Distinguished Service Cross to the undermentioned officer:—
LG 4.6.1917 p 5462

- Asst. Payr. Lawrence William Williams, RNR

LG 15.6.1917 pp 5955/7

Admiralty,
15th June 1917.
The following despatch has been received from the Commander in Chief, Cape of Good Hope Station, describing the later coastal operations by HM ships against German East Africa:—

HMS "Hyacinth"
28th January 1917.
Sir, Be pleased to lay before their Lordships the following report of the later coastal operations against German East Africa by HM ships under my orders.
These operations may be said to have commenced with the occupation, on the 1st

August 1916, of the town of Saadani by naval forces, assisted by a detachment of the Zanzibar African Rifles. The capture of this coast town was undertaken at the request of General Smuts, and was well and effectively carried out under the immediate supervision of Captain A. H. Williamson, MVO, of "Vengeance" (flying my flag) for the outer squadron, and of Captain E. J. A. Fullerton, DSO, of "Severn" for the inshore squadron; Commander R. J. N. Watson of "Vengeance", being in command of the landing party.

The force was landed in boats from "Vengeance", "Talbot", (Captain R. C. Kemble Lambert DSO), "Severn", and "Mersey", (Commander R. A. Wilson, DSO) about one mile to the north of the town at 6 am, "Severn" and "Mersey" covering the landing with their guns. But slight opposition was experienced, only three casualties being sustained. The fort was enclosed in a boma, which had been constructed originally to keep out leopards and savages, and was surrounded by the native village and dense bush, which had to be cleared.

During the period of naval occupation a few encounters took place between our advanced patrols and those of the enemy, but no attack in force was made and our energies were confined to consolidating the position.

On the 5th August, the whole of the naval forces, except the Marines and a few special details, re-embarked on military forces being landed to relieve them.

On the 13th August I received a wireless message from the military officer in command at Saadani, giving the enemy force at Bagamoyo at about ten whites and forty Askaris, and asking if the Navy would take the town, as its earliest occupation was essential, I replied that this would be done and issued orders accordingly.

Although the information given me indicated that the enemy force was small, I knew that it would be strongly entrenched, and would have Maxims, and I therefore decided to land what force I could raise from the ships immediately available, together with all machine guns, and to have a strong covering force of light draught ships inshore with heavy draught ships outside. As it turned out the intelligence was very much at fault, the enemy havine one 4.1 in. gun, one five barrelled pom pom, and two Maxims, their total force being more numerous than the landing party.

At 5 pm on the 14th August, "Vengeance", (Flag) with "Challenger", (Captain A. C. Sykes)

and "Manica" (Commander W. E. Whittingham, RNR) in company, left Zanzibar, anchoring at 3.24 am on the 15th off Bagamoyo, the landing party leaving "Vengeance" at 4.40 am under the command of Commander R. J. N. Watson. There was a slight swell, little wind, and a bright moon, so that a complete surprise was not to be expected; but the landing turned out to be as near a surprise as was possible in the circumstances, and it is believed that the boats were not seen until they had left the monitors at 5.30 am.

Owing to the skill with which the advance was conducted by Commander Watson and Commander (acting) W. B. Wilkinson, and an alteration of course when some little way from the shore, the enemy were completely deceived as to the point of landing, and found themselves under a heavy fire from the monitors and motor boats, which effectually prevented them from firing on the landing party.

The latter proceeded and landed close under the 4.1 in. gun position to the left of the town, at a point where the gun, owing to its position some 30 feet back from the ridge on which it was sited, could not be sufficiently depressed to bear on them.

On the other hand this gun came under the enfilading fire of the 3 pounders, one each in my steam barge, Vengeance's picket boat, and the tug "Helmuth". This fire, at from 800 to 500 yards, so seriously discomposed the enemy that they abandoned the gun as soon as attacked by the shore party. This gun had come from Tanga in tow of 500 coolies, and had arrived at the position in which it was taken on the 9th August. Its capture was, in my opinion, a most remarkable piece of work, reflecting the greatest credit on the boats and the attacking section.

Meanwhile the "Manica" had got up her kite balloon and was spotting, but her seaplane had engine trouble and was forced to come down in the breakers at the mouth of the Kingani River, returning undamaged. I accordingly called on "Himalaya" (Captain Colin Mackenzie, DSO), which was just leaving Zanzibar, and at 6am her seaplane flew across from Zanzibar, and at once dropped bombs on the enemy in trenches, afterwards spotting. "Himalaya" herself followed and took a useful part in the subsequent bombardment.

At 6.30 am it was reported from three sources – kite, balloon, portable W/T set ashore and W/T from seaplane – that the enemy were retiring between the French Mission and the sea, and were around the Mission.

The cause of this retreat was the endeavour of Captain von Bok to rush his troops round to the opposite side of town to oppose our landing. About this time the pom pom gun was hit by a 6 in. shell from "Severn" (Commander (acting) W. B. C. Jones) and nearly pulverised, Captain von Boedecke being killed. Shortly after Captain von Bok was also killed, and with both leaders gone all initiative on the part of the enemy was lost, and our men were able to firmly establish themselves in a small but important quarter of the town, from which they subsequently spread and gathered in all the Arabs, Indians and natives. Beyond slight damage from shell fire and a fire in the native village – where an occasional fire is beneficial – the town is intact.

The importance of the capture of this town on the native mind was very great, as it is the old capital of the slave trade and the starting place of the great caravan routes into the interior.

The result from a military point of view was immediately apparent in the demoralisation of the enemy forces, particularly the native portion, and in the evacuation of the Mtoni Ferry, a strategic and strongly defended position about six miles above the town over the Kingani River, thereby giving our troops moving south from Saadani and Mandera an open road.

It is with deep regret that I record the death of Captain Francis H. Thomas, DSC, Royal Marine Light Infantry, whilst gallantly leading his men. He had taken part in all recent operations and was a most promising officer. Our other casualties were two seamen and two marines wounded, while the Zanzibar African Rifles had one sergeant and one Askari killed and one Askari wounded. Two native porters were also wounded.

The enemy casualties were estimated at two officers, one white soldier, and eight Askaris killed, three white and eight Askaris wounded, and four white and fifteen Askaris taken prisoner.

On the 20th August, the naval forces were relieved by the Military and re-embarked in their ships.

On the 21st August, in continuance of the policy of harassing Dar-es-Salaam, "Vengeance" and "Challenger" bombarded various gun positions; and during that night "Challenger" carried out a further bombardment, firing 50 rounds of 6 in. over the town into the railway station. On the 23rd, 26th, 28th, 30th and 31st

August, and on the 1st September, other limited bombardments took place, and on the 3rd September the whalers "Pickle" (Lieutenant H. C. Davis, DSC, RD, RNR) "Fly" (Lieutenant D. H. H. Whitburn, RNR) "Childers" (Lieutenant V. C. Large, RNR) and "Echo" (Lieutenant C. J. Charlewood, DSC, RNR), under Flag Commander the Hon. R. O. B. Bridgeman, DSO, simulated a landing at Upanga and attacked the front at short range from West Ferry Point to Ras Upanga. They were received with shrapnel fire from a field battery but escaped injury.

Meanwhile preparations for the advance on Dar-es-Salaam were in full swing, and on the 31st August the military advance started from Bagamoyo, the main body marching south and being strongly reinforced at Konduchi on the 2nd September, for which landing they themselves formed the covering party. The plan succeeded admirably, the enemy retiring and making little attempt to oppose the advance, so that in the end the final reinforcements actually landed in face of the very formidable entrenchments at Mssassani Bay.

With the military column went six naval maxims, six Lewis guns, one 3 pounder Hotchkiss on field mounting, and a medical section, the party being under the command of Commander H. D. Bridges, DSO, of Hyacinth. Communication between the main column and the small craft inshore was maintained by a naval wireless party.

The march of 36 miles proved exceedingly arduous, the road turning into little better than a sandy track through a waterless district. Porters were short and speedily dropped behind with provisions, to add to which the first regiment of African descent which arrived at Mssassani consumed the 12,000 gallons of water and three days provisions for the whole force.

On the 3rd September, following on the simulated landing from the whalers, a brisk bombardment of gun positions to the northward of the town, and in advance of our troops, was carried out for half an hour until 7 am, when firing ceased and our troops continued their advance to the outskirts of the town.

As matters now appeared ripe to demand the surrender of the town, on the morning of the 4th September, "Challenger", flying a white flag, proceeded to Makatumbe with a written demand, signed by me and by the Officer commanding troops. This was transferred to the "Echo", which took it as far as the boom and then sent it ashore in her boat.

About 8 am the deputy burgomaster, the bank manager, and an interpreter came off in the "Echo", and agreed to the conditions of the demand, giving all the required guarantees. Our troops were at once told by wireless to advance into the town. All ships entered Dar-es-Salaam Bay, and during the afternoon the monitors entered the harbour after destroying the hawsers of the boom across the entrance.

I landed with my staff at 2.30 pm and at 3 o'clock the Union Jack was hoisted over the Magistracy with full honours.

Following on the occupation of Dar-es-Salaam, it became necessary to seize other coast towns further south, and thus prevent the enemy from retreating by the coast to Lindi and the southern ports.

In consequence, on the 7th September, a simultaneous attack was made on the two Kilwas (Kivinje and Kisiwani) with the object of getting possession of these towns and holding the two hills, Singino Hill and Mpara Hill, which command Kilwa Kivinje and Port Beaver respectively. After four 12 in. shrapnel had been placed on the top of Singino Hill by "Vengeance", a white man was seen endeavouring to haul down the German colours at Kivinje and to hoist his boy's white kanzu in their place. This was observed just in time to prevent fire being opened from "Vengeance" with 6 in. guns on the trenches along the beach. A flag of truce was sent in, the town surrendered unconditionally, and a force was landed and occupied the town and the hill. Meanwhile Kilwa Kisiwani had surrendered unconditionally to "Talbot" who landed a party and occupied Mpara Hill.

Operations against the three Southern Ports of Mikindani, Sudi and Lindi commenced on the 13th September, when 200 Marines, 700 Indian troops, 200 Zanzibar and Mafia African Rifles, 12 naval machine guns, 2 hotchkiss guns and 950 porters were landed at Mikindani in boats from "Vengeance", "Talbot", "Himalaya", and "Princess". (Captain C. La P. Lewin), assisted by the gunboats "Thistle" (Commander Hector Boyes) and "Rinaldo" (Lieut. Cdr. H. M. Garrett), and the kite balloon ship "Manica" and the transport "Barjora". There was no opposition, and the town was occupied by 9 am.

On the 14th September our troops commenced their advance towards Sudi, while "Vengeance", Hyacinth, "Talbot", and "Himalaya" with "Barjora", proceeded round to the anchorage

outside there. Whalers entered the inner harbour at daylight on the 16th, experiencing no resistance.

The whole force, having left a garrison of 100 men at Mikindani, marched to Sudi, arriving there at noon, when the marines, naval guns and African Rifles were embarked, the intention being to land these as a covering party outside Lindi under the guns of the squadron, while the main force marched from Sudi to Lindi, where, if any resistance was put up, they would have held a commanding position on the south side of the river.

Early on the 16th the ships proceeded to Lindi Bay and the Naval Brigade was landed after a short bombardment of the selected beach with 6 in guns. An attempt to send in a flag of truce was made, but no answer could be obtained, and from seaplane observations the town appeared to be deserted. Supported by "Thistle", the force advanced along the beach and occupied the town.

The troops who were thus saved a long and arduous march from Sudi to Lindi, were re-embarked at Sudi on the evening of the 16th, leaving a garrison of 100 men there. They arrived at Lindi on the 17th and relieved the Naval Brigade and African Rifles, who were re-embarked.

The same evening, "Talbot", "Thistle" and "Barjora", with a detachment of Indian troops on board, left Lindi, and by 8 am on the 18th, Kiswere was occupied without any opposition, the troops remaining as a garrison.

This was the last town of any importance on the coast of German East Africa, and the whole coast line is now occupied with the exception of the Rufiji Delta.

In connection with the operations covered by this despatch I append a list of officers and men whom I specially desire to bring to the notice of their Lordships for meritorious services.

I have the honour to be, Sir,
Your obedient servant,
(Signed) E. Charlton,
Rear Admiral,
Commander in Chief.

The Distinguished Service Cross has been awarded to the undermentioned Officers in recognition of their services in the operations described in the Commander in Chief's despatch:—
LG 15.6.1917 p 5959

- Lieut. Eldred Stuart Brooksmith, RN
Was in sole command of the defences of the southern part of the defence lines at Bagamoyo, when he showed conspicuous ability; also contributed largely to the successful firing by the monitors.
- Flight Lieutenant James Edward Baker Maclean, RNAS.
Since April 1916 has carried out constant flights over the enemy's coast, including reconnaissances, bomb dropping and spotting, was wounded when flying over Bagamoyo.
- Mr. John Mackay, Chief Gunner, RN.
Was in command of whaler Salamander, and did excellent work under fire; organised minesweeping with great efficiency.

The KING has further approved of the following awards of the Distinguished Service Cross to the undermentioned Officers in recognition of their services with the East African Military Forces:—
LG 15.6.1917 p 5959

- Squadron Commander Eric Roper Curzon Nanson, RNAS
Organised his unit with great efficiency and zeal, and carried out reconnaissance work under great climatic difficulties.
- Lieutenant Vincent Holland Pryor Molteno, RN.
Organised the naval gun detachment which he commanded during part of the Kibata operations.
- Flight Sub. Lieut. Leslie O. Brown.
For bravery, zeal and ability shown in many long flights over enemy territory on reconnaissance work and bomb dropping expeditions; was repeatedly under fire.
- Flt. Lieut. Norman Gordon Stewart-Dawson.
Carried out reconnaissance over difficult country on 30th May 1916 when he was obliged to land in the bush.
- Lieut. William John King, RNVR.
For continuous good service in the operations of the Umba Valley Field Force; also served as Assistant Transport Officer and as Port Captain, Tanga.
- Captain Ernest William O'Connor, Master of Transport, Barjora.
Showed exceptional ability in the coast operations, the success of the landings being largely due to his professional capacity and zeal.

The KING has been graciously pleased to approve of the award of the Distinguished Service Cross to the undermentioned Officers:—

LG 22.6.1917 p 6254

- Lieut. Hugh Evelyn Raymond, RN
- Lieut. Reginald Nash, RN
- Lieut. Edward Arthur Aylmer, RN
- Lieut. Colin John Lawrence Bittleston, RN
- Lieut. Leonard Ernest Pearson, RN
- Act. Lieut. Edward Lyon Berthon, RN
- Lieut. William Stanley Nelson, RNR
- Lieut. Hugh Ross Mackay, RNR
- Lieut. John Joseph Fulton, RNR
- Lieut. Nelson Cooper, RNR
- Lieut. Richard James Turnbull, RNR
- Eng. Lieut. Alexander Kenny, RNR
- Lieut. Robert Alexander Paterson, RNVR
- Sub. Lieut. James Henry Arnold, RNR
- Sub. Lieut. Clarence Aubrey King, RNVR
- Skipper Thomas Edward Cain, RNR, 2061, WSA.
- Skipper William Henry Brewer, RNR, 2440, SA
- Skipper William Arthur Mead, RNR, 1518, SA.
- Skipper Adam Forbes, RNR, 66, WSA
The following Officer has been awarded a Bar to the Distinguished Service Cross for a subsequent act of gallantry:—
- Lieut. Frederick Henry Peterson, DSO, DSC, RNR
(The award of the Distinguished Service Cross was announced in *London Gazette* dated 14th July 1916).

The KING has been graciously pleased to approve of the award of the Distinguished Service Cross to the undermentioned officers:
LG 22.6.1917 pp 6255/7

- Flt. Cdr. Philip Leslie Holmes, RNAS
- Flt. Sub. Lieut. (now act. Flt. Cdr) Herbert Gardner Travers, RNAS
In recognition of his services with the Army in France. This Officer has himself brought down three hostile aeroplanes completely out of control, and has taken part in two other combats in which enemy machines were forced to land in our lines. He has always shown the greatest determination in leading his flight on offensive patrols, and has on many occasions driven down superior numbers of hostile machines.
- Flt. Lieut. Edward J. Cooper, RNAS.
- Flt. Sub. Lieut. Charles Reginald Morrish, RNAS
- Flt. Sub. Lieut. Henry George Boswell, RNAS
- Flt. Lieut. Charles Langston Scott, RNAS
- Flt. Lieut. Walter Travers Swire Williams, RNAS
- Flt. Lieut. Thomas Grey Culling, RNAS
In recognition of his services on the 23rd April 1917, when with two other machines he engaged a formation of nine hostile scouts and

two seater machines. Two two seater machines were shot down, one of them by Flt. Lieut. Culling unassisted.

- Flt. Lieut. Francis Dominic Casey, RNAS
For conspicuous bravery and skill in attacking hostile aircraft on numerous occasions. On April 21st 1917, he attacked a hostile two seater machine at a range varying from 40 – 100 yards, and brought it down completely out of control. On April 23rd, 1917, on four different occasions during one flight, he attacked hostile machines, one of which was driven down in a spinning nose dive and another turning over on its side went down completely out of control. This Officer has driven down four machines completely out of control, and forced many others down.
- Flt. Lieut. Charles Adrian Maitland-Heriot, RNAS.
- Flt. Sub. Lieut. John Roland Secretan Devlin, RNAS
- Sub. Lieut. Rupert Forbes Bentley, RNVR
In recognition of their services in a bombing attack on the Kuleli Burgas Bridge on 4th January 1917, when several direct hits were scored and considerable damage done. The machines were exposed to anti-aircraft, rifle and machine gun fire during the attack, and also on the return journey.
- Flt. Sub. Lieut. Leo Philip Paine, RNAS
- Flt. Sub. Lieut. Robert Leckie, RNAS
- Flt. Sub. Lieut. Basil Deacon Hobbs, RNAS
- Flt. Sub. Lieut. Charles McNicoll, RNAS
- Flt. Sub. Lieut. Valentine Edgar Sieveking, RNAS
In recognition of his services on the night of 3rd to 4th May 1917, when he dropped bombs on Ostend seaplane base with good results, making two trips.
- Flt. Sub. Lieut. Harold Thomas Mellings, RNAS
In recognition of his services on the 19th March 1917, when he attacked a hostile aeroplane with great gallantry at heights varying from 12,000 to 2,000 feet.
- Flt. Sub. Lieut. Frederick Earle Fraser, RNAS
- Flt. Lieut. (act. Flt. Cdr) Charles Dawson Booker.
For special gallantry in the field on numerous occasions, especially the following:—
On 26th April 1917, he went to the assistance of some of our photographic machines, which were about to be attacked by twelve Albatross scouts. One of these he fired on at close range, and brought it down out of control.
On 24th May 1917, whilst on patrol, he went to the assistance of a formation of our machines, which was being attacked by nine hostile

scouts. He attacked one of the latter, which was driven down in flames and crashed. Later in the same day he attacked and drove down out of control another hostile machine.
On numerous other occasions he has attacked enemy machines and driven them down out of control.
- Flt. Lieut. George Goodman Simpson.
For gallantry and able leadership in aerial fighting, notably on the following occasions:—
On 3rd May 1917 he drove down a hostile aeroplane out of control.
On 11th May 1917, while on offensive patrol with five other machines, he attacked six hostile aircraft. One of these he brought down out of control, and a few minutes later he attacked another at close range and brought it down in flames.
On 23rd May 1917 he led a formation of five machines to attack at least twice that number of hostile aeroplanes. Both formations became split up, and a general fight ensued. Five times during the combat he drove off hostile aeroplanes from another of our machines, and one of those which he attacked was seen to go down in a spin.

The undermentioned Officers have been awarded a Bar to the Distinguished Service Cross for subsequent acts of gallantry:—
- Flt. Cdr. Theodore Douglas Hallam, DSC, RNAS (The award of the Distinguished Service Cross was announced in the *London Gazette* of 15th December 1915).
- Flt. Cdr. Roderic Stanley Dallas, DSC, RNAS
In recognition of his services on the 23rd April 1917, when with two other machines he engaged a formation of nine hostile scouts and two seater machines. Two two seater machines were shot down, one of them by Flt. Cdr. Dallas unassisted.
(The award of the Distinguished Service Cross was announced in the *London Gazette* of 6th September 1916).
- Flt. Lieut. Charles Langston Scott, DSC, RNAS.
- Flt. Lieut. Robert Alexander Little, DSC, RNAS
For exceptional daring and skill in aerial fighting on many occasions, of which the following are examples:—
On the 28th April 1917 he destroyed an Aviatik; on the 29th April he shot down a hostile scout, which crashed. On the 30th April, with three other machines he went up after hostile machines and saw a big fight going on between fighter escorts and hostile aircraft. Flt. Lieut. Little attacked one at fifty yards range, and brought it down out of control. A few minutes later he attacked a red scout with a

larger machine than the rest. This machine was handled with great skill, but by clever manoeuvring, Flt. Lieut. Little got into a good position and shot it down out of control. (The award of the Distinguished Service Cross was announced in the *London Gazette* of 16th February 1917).

The KING has been graciously pleased to approve the award of the Distinguished Service Cross to the undermentioned Officers of the British Mercantile Marine, in recognition of zeal and devotion to duty shown in carrying on the trade of the country during the war:—
LG 22.6.1917 p 6257

- Capt. William Frodsom
- Capt. Stanley Cooper

The KING has been graciously pleased to give orders for the award of the Distinguished Service Cross to the undermentioned officers in recognition of their services in vessels of the Auxilliary Patrol between the 1st February and 31st December 1916:—
LG 27.6.1917 pp 6377/8

- Lieut. Walter Stafford, RNR
- Lieut. Ronald James Mortimer, RNR
- Lieut. Norman Baker, RNR
- Lieut. John Henry Holman, RNR
- Lieut. David Jefferson, RNR
- Lieut. George Walker, RNR
- Lieut. Ernest Victor Hugo, RNR
- Lieut. Alfred Henry Barnes, RNR
- Lieut. Alfred Sand Holmes, RNR
- Lieut. William Henry Askew Bee, RNR
- Lieut. Geoffrey Messenger, RNR
- Lieut. Edward Lewis Owen, RNR
- Lieut. Edward Wilkinson, RNR
- Lieut. John Trewhella Rowe, RNR
- Lieut. Tom Turnbull Laurenson, RNR
- Lieut. Alfred George Dodman, RNR
- Lieut. Gordon William Hatchard Lyndon, RNR
- Lieut. John Williams le Boutillier, RNR
- Lieut. Henry Jones, RNR
- Lieut. Richard Stephens Durham, RNR
- Lieut. Gordon Murray Croal Thomson, RNR
- Lieut. James Hogg Reid, RNR
- Lieut. Henry Brodie Conby, RNR
- Lieut. John Noble Day, RNR
- Lieut. Lawrence Peel Massy, RNR
- Lieut. Edward Horrabin Clements, RNR
- Act. Lieut. Robert Henry Baunton, RNR
- Act. Lieut. Ben Chaplin, RNR
- Lieut. Norman Graham Croall, RNVR
- Lieut. Lionel Sheard Chappell, RNVR

- Ch. Skipper Frederick Ernest Willis, RNR 1615 WSA
- Ch. Skipper William Alfred Capps, RNR 1796 WSA
- Skipper Alexander Bruce Summers, RNR 1048 WSA
- Skipper John Bruce, RNR 1331 WSA
- Skipper James Cutter, RNR 833 DA
- Skipper William Bramwell Jenner, RNR 1848 WSA
- Skipper John Samuel Macey, RNR 497 WSA
- Skipper Thomas Turner, RNR 664 WSA
- Skipper William Henry Sweet, RNR 2134 WSA

The KING has been graciously pleased to give orders for the award of the Distinguished Service Cross to the undermentioned officers in recognition of their services in Minesweeping operations between the 1st July 1916 and the 31st March 1917:—
LG 2.7.1917 pp 6519/20

- Lieut. William Victor Rice, DSO, RN
- Lieut. Claude Preston Hermon-Hodge, RN
- Lieut. Arthur Perfect Meredith Lewes, RN
- Lieut. William Dene Keith Dowding, RN
- Lieut. Archibald Henry L. S. Ruddell, RN
- Lieut. Ebenezer Gordon, RNR
- Lieut. Edward L. Dobson, RNR
- Lieut. John H Pitts, RNR
- Lieut. Alfred Havercroft Chafer, RNR
- Lieut. Howard McGlashan, RNR
- Lieut. Percy Noble Taylor, RNR
- Lieut. George B. Musson, RNR
- Lieut. Eric Rees, RNR
- Lieut. Charles Sidney Mence, RNR
- Lieut. Arthur Sandison, RNR
- Lieut. Wilfrid Walter Storey, RNR
- Lieut. Benjamin Swinhoe Stothard, RNR
- Lieut. Fred Collins, RNR
- Lieut. Thomas Elliott Hodge, RNR
- Lieut. Francis Joseph Woods, RNR
- Lieut. Roxburghe Tulloch, RNR
- Lieut. Alexander Duff Thomson, RNR
- Lieut. Iann Mackenzie Adie, RNR
- Eng. Lieut. Joseph Hall, RNR
- Act. Lieut. John Williams Powell, RNR
- Act. Lieut. Alexander Finlayson, RNR
- Act. Lieut. Charles Frederick Le Patourel, RNR
- Act. Lieut. Bernard Lawson Parker, RNR
- Act. Lieut. Percy Ridley, RNR
- Skipper Alexander McLeod, RNR 759 SA
- Skipper George Mair, RNR 770 SA
- Skipper Francis Thompson, RNR 54 SA
- Skipper John Yolland, RNR 58 WSA
- Skipper Horace Edward Nutten, RNR 60 SA
- Skipper Thomas Reid, RNR 490 WSA
- Skipper James Edward Calvert, RNR 767 WSA

- Skipper Robert Barker, RNR 843 WSA
- Skipper Samuel Beach Ward, RNR 1369 WSA
- Skipper George Gill, RNR 1979 WSA

The KING has been graciously pleased to approve of the award of the Distinguished Service Cross to the undermentioned Officers:—
LG 20.7.1917 p 7423

- Lieut. (now Lieut. Cdr) Edward Bernard Cornish Dicken, RN
- Asst. Payr (Act Payr) Victor Cecil Gould Eason, RN
For services on the Staff of the Vice Admiral commanding the Eastern Mediterranean Squadron, between June 1916 and June 1917.
- Lieut. John Jenkins, RNR
For services in command of a seaplane carrying vessel, on the East Indies and Egypt Station during the period 1st April 1916 – 31st March 1917.
- Lieut. John Kerr, RNR.
For services in command of a seaplane carrying vessel on the East Indies and Egypt Station during the period 1st April 1916 to 31st March 1917.
- Sub. Lieut. (Act Lieut) Henry Beattie Bell-Irving, RNVR
In recognition of his services in command of HM Drifter, I.F.S., in an engagement with five enemy seaplanes on the 11th June 1917. Two of the enemy machines were brought down by gunfire and destroyed.

The KING has been graciously pleased to approve of the award of the Distinguished Service Cross to Officers and men for services in action with enemy submarines.
LG 20.7.1917 p 7424

- Flt. Lieut. John Edward Alfred Hoare, RNAS
- Lieut. Peter Shaw, RNR
- Lieut. Charles William Walters, RNR
- Lieut. Herbert Lionel Upton, RNR
- Lieut. Peter Nicholson, RNR
- Lieut. Charles George Bonner, RNR
- Flt. Sub. Lieut. William Louis Anderson, RNAS
- Sub. Lieut. Keith Morris, RNR
- Skipper John Kime, RNR 670 WSA
- Skipper George Hubert Cecil Gray, RNR 1558 WSA
- Skipper Harry Gower, RNR 1845 WSA
- Skipper John Watson, RNR 920 SA

To receive a Bar to the Distinguished Service Cross.
- Lieut. William Geoffrey Messenger, DSC, RNR
- Act. Lieut. Richard Percy Nisbet, DSC, RNR

- Asst. Payr. Reginald Arthur Nunn, DSC, RNR

The KING has been graciously pleased to approve of the award of the Distinguished Service Cross to the undermentioned Officers:—
LG 20.7.1917 pp 7424/5

- Flt. Cdr. John Callaghan Brooke, RNAS.
In recognition of his services in the East Indies and Egypt Seaplane Squadron during the period 1st April 1916 – 31st March 1917. During this time he took part in several valuable reconnaissances and bombing flights, obtaining important information and doing considerable damage to enemy organisations.
- Flt. Cdr. Thomas Francis Netterville Gerrard, RNAS.
In recognition of his services during an air fight on the 4th June 1917. This officer led his flight against 15-20 hostile aeroplanes, and alone had ten engagements with these machines.
He attacked one and fired sixty rounds into its cockpit at point blank range, the enemy machine rolling over and over for 3,000 feet and then falling vertically out of control.
He then attacked another enemy machine which had dived on to one of our machines from behind, and with the help of a Scout he shot it down, the enemy being seen to crash to the ground.
Another hostile scout was then attacked by pilot, end on, and received a long burst at very close range, the enemy going down in a spin, but apparently righting himself lower down. During this last encounter, Flt. Cdr. Gerrard's machine was riddled with bullets, but by fine piloting, he landed safely, although all but his lateral controls were shot away and his machine damaged to such an extent as to require return to Depot for complete re-building.
This officer has now destroyed at least seven hostile aircraft. He was on active service in France and Belgium from April to September 1916, and during that period performed much valuable work.
- Flt. Cdr. Reginald Frederick Stuart Leslie, RNAS.
In recognition of his gallantry in pursuing hostile raiding aeroplanes out to sea in a land machine on the 25th May 1917. He attacked one hostile aeroplane, and caused it to descend in a steep nose dive, emitting smoke and steam. He was unable to observe its fate, as he was himself immediately attacked from behind by two other hostile machines and temporarily lost control. When he regained control, the machine which he had first attacked had

disappeared, and two others were proceeding eastwards at a considerable height above him. He then returned safely to his aerodrome.

- Flt. Lieut. Guy Duncan Smith, RNAS
In recognition of his services in the East Indies and Egypt Seaplane Squadron during the period 1st April 1916 to 31st March 1917. During this time he took part in several valuable reconnaissances and bombing flights, obtaining important information and doing considerable damage to enemy organisations.

- Flt. Lieut. Raymond Collishaw, RNAS.
In recognition of his services on various occasions, especially the following: On June 1st, 1917, this officer shot down an Albatross Scout in flames.
On 3rd June 1917, he shot down an Albatross Scout in flames. On 5th June 1917, he shot down a two seater Albatross in flames. On the 6th June 1917, he shot down two Albatross scouts in flames and killed the pilot in a third. He has displayed great gallantry and skill in all his combats.

- Flt. Sub. Lieut. Norman Richard Cook, RNAS
For his services in an air raid on Zeebrugge Mole and hostile shipping, on the 27th of May 1917.

- Flt. Sub. Lieut. Robert Frederick Lea Dickey, RNAS.

- Warrt. Offr. (2nd Gr) Frank Henry Whitmore, RNAS.
In recognition of his services in the East Indies and Egypt Seaplane Squadron during the period 1st April 1916 to 31st March 1917.

The KING has been graciously pleased to approve the award of the Distinguished Service Gross to the undermentioned Officers of the British Mercantile Marine, in recognition of zeal and devotion to duty shown in carrying on the trade of the country during the war:-
LG 20.7.1917 p 7425

- Capt. Arthur Matravers King
- Capt. Ernest Stanley Hutchinson
- Capt. John McLelland
- Capt. John Prideaux
- Ch. Engr. Robert Bay

To receive a Bar to the Distinguished Service Cross.
- Capt. David Philip McDonald.

The following awards of the Distinguished Service Cross have been approved.
LG 11.8.1917 p 8204.

- Lieut. William Edward Senior, RNR

In recognition of his services in minesweeping operations between the 1st July 1916, and the 31st March 1917.

- Sub. Lieut. Alistair Gordon Cameron, RNR
For his services in oversea submarines in enemy waters during 1915-16.

- Lieut. Wright Charles Walter Ingle, RNVR
For services with a Naval Armoured Car Squadron in France, Belgium, Turkey and Romania. On the 2nd December 1916 he showed conspicuous gallantry and devotion to duty when his car was bogged and his leg was shattered by a bullet whilst he was for the second time starting up the engine. He took refuge in a shell hole and crawled back to the Russian trenches on his back during the night, taking twelve hours to accomplish the distance.

- Lieut. Edwin Follett, RNVR.
- Lieut. Edward Corfrae Ruft D'Eye, RNVR
- Sub. Lieut. (now Lieut) Robert Cowley, RNVR
- Sub. Lieut. Stanley Webber, RNVR
- Engr (now Eng. Lieut. Cdr) George Harold Hindman, RIM
- Lieut. Henry Philip Hughes-Hallet, RIM
- Lieut. Albane Rahere Castleton Poyntz, RIM
- Lieut. Cecil Gwydyr Hallett, RIM
- Lieut. Harold Townshend Boultbee, RIM
- Lieut. Charles Jacomb Nicoll, RIM
- Lieut. Isaac John Duncan, RIM
- Lieut. Thomas Joseph Farrell, RIM (now Capt. RE)
- Lieut. Joseph Noel Metcalfe, RIM (now Capt. RE)
- Sub. Lieut. Arcel Price Llewellyn, RIM
In recognition of zeal, devotion to duty and gallantry whilst serving in River Steamers for long periods during the operations in Mesopotamia.

- Capt. Samuel Davison, Mercantile Marine.
For the conspicuous zeal and gallantry which he displayed on discovering an enemy mine. Capt. Davison took steps to warn shipping of the possible presence of a minefield, and towed the mine for several miles out of the route of traffic. He then remained secured to the moorings of the mine until one of HM ships arrived on the scene when he actively assisted in the recovery of the mine.

The KING has been graciously pleased to approve of the award of the Distinguished Service Cross to Officers for services in action with enemy submarines:-
LG 11.8.1917 pp 8205/6

- Flt. Lieut. Warren Rawson Mackenzie, RNAS
- Lieut. Reginald Charles Butler, RNR
- Lieut. Henry Johnson, RNR

- Lieut. John Pollok, RNR
- Lieut. George Leslie, RNR
- Lieut. John Kerr (b) RNR
- Lieut. Thomas Hughes, RNR
- Engr. Lieut. James Burns, RNR
- Lieut. John Charles Jones, RNVR

To Receive a Bar to the Distinguished Service Cross.
- Flt. Sub. Lieut. Richard Frederick Lea Dickey, DSC, RNAS

The KING has been graciously pleased to approve of the award of the Distinguished Service Cross to the undermentioned Officers:-
LG 11.8.1917 p 8207

- Flt. Cdr. Alexander Macdonald Shook, RNAS
- Flt. Lieut. Arnold Jaques Chadwick, RNAS (since reported drowned)
- Flt. Sub. Lieut. Albert James Enstone, RNAS
- Flt. Sub. Lieut. Langley Frank Willard Smith, RNAS (since missing).
  For exceptional gallantry and remarkable skill and courage whilst serving with the RNAS at Dunkirk during May and June 1917, in repeatedly attacking and destroying hostile aircraft.
- Flt. Lieut. Cecil Hill Darley, RNAS.
  For conspicuous skill and gallantry on the night of the 2nd July 1917. One of his engines having seized whilst he was over Bruges, he dropped his bombs on the objective and managed to fly his machine home on one engine and effected a safe landing on the aerodrome.
- Flt. Sub. Lieut. (now Flt. Lieut) John Edward Scott, RNAS.
  For the skill and gallantry with which he engaged a hostile machine returning from an air raid on England. Descending to 8,000 feet, he fired continuously until the enemy machine lost control, descended in a spinning nose dive and crashed into the sea.
- Flt. Sub. Lieut. Ellis Vair Reid, RNAS (since missing).
  In recognition of his services on the following occasions:—
  On the 6th June 1917, he attacked and drove down one of four hostile scouts. This machine dived nose first into the ground and was destroyed.
  On the afternoon of the 15th June 1917, he was leading a patrol of three scouts and encountered a formation of ten enemy machines. During the combat which ensued he forced one machine down completely out of control. Next he attacked at a range of about 30 yards another hostile scout. The pilot of this

machine was killed, and it went down completely out of control.
This Officer has at all times shown the greatest bravery and determination.
- Flt. Sub. Lieut. Edward Robert Barker, RNAS
  In recognition of his services on the occasion of an air raid on the Solway works at Zeebrugge on the night of the 15th-16th July 1917, when bombs were dropped on the objective with good results.
- Flt. Sub. Lieut. Rowan Heywood Daly, RNAS
  For skill and gallantry in attacking enemy aircraft returning from a raid on England. After a long chase he engaged and brought down one machine in flames. Afterwards he engaged a second machine, but his gun jammed and though he continued the pursuit to the enemy coast, he failed to clear the jam and was obliged to return to his aerodrome.
- Flt. Lieut. Reginald Rhys Soar, RNAS
  For courage and skill as a scout pilot. On 23rd May 1917, he attacked a two seater artillery machine, and as the result of a well thought out attack brought the machine down out of control.
  On 12th June 1917 he brought down two enemy machines out of control.
  On 29th June 1917 in company with Flt. Lieut. Little, he attacked and brought down an Albatross scout.
  On 3rd July 1917, whilst leading an offensive patrol, a formation of seven Albatross Scouts was engaged, and he brought down one out of control.
  On 13th July 1917, in company with Flt. Lieut. Little, he attacked and drove down out of control one two seater machine following it down to within 1,000 feet of the ground.

To receive a Bar to the Distinguished Service Cross.
- Flt. Cdr. Robert John Orton Compston, DSC, RNAS
  For gallantry in action and for very good work in driving away German artillery aeroplanes.
  On the 12th June 1917, with three other machines, he attacked six hostile scouts. He got close to one, and shot it down out of control.
  On the 16th June 1917, he attacked and brought down a two seater Aviatik.
  On the 3rd July 1917, he attacked two Aviatiks, which he drove down and forced to land.
- Flt. Lieut. John Edward Sharman, DSC, RNAS
  For courage and skill in attacking enemy aircraft. On the evening of the 14th June 1917, while on an offensive patrol with three other scouts, he observed five Albatross Scouts. He dived on one of these, firing from his machine-

gun at about 50 feet range. The Scout then went down in a spin.

On the 24th June 1917, with six other machines, he attacked fifteen Albatross Scouts. After a combat at close range he destroyed one of these, its right plane and tail plane falling off.

The KING has been graciously pleased to approve of the award of the Distinguished Service Cross to the undermentioned Officers of the British Mercantile Marine, in recognition of zeal and devotion to duty shown in carrying on the trade of the country during the war:—
LG 11.8.1917 p 8208.

- Capt. George McDonald Dobbie
- Capt. David Lawton
- Capt. Robert George James
- Capt. Walter Gay
- Capt. Frederick Douglas Struss
- Ch. Offr. Alexander Smith
- Ch. Engr. William Russell Stobo

The KING has been graciously pleased to give orders for the award of the decorations specified below to the undermentioned officers in recognition of their services in the action in the Straits of Otranto on the 15th May 1917:—
LG 29.8.1917 pp 8985/6

To receive the Distinguished Service Cross:—
- Skipper William Bruce, RNR 1486 WSA
  He remained at his post with his crew when under the fire of a very superior force until his ship HM Drifter "Quarry Knowe", blew up.
- Skipper Robert Stephen, RNR 1384, WSA.
  He remained at his post, although under heavy fire from a very superior force, until his ship, HM Drifter "Taits" was badly damaged and in a sinking condition.
- Skipper William Farquhar, RNR 1310, WSA
  He remained at his post with his crew although under the fire of a very superior force, only leaving his ship HM Drifter "Admirable", as she was sinking.
- Skipper Robert Cowe, RNR 1774 WSA
  Although under fire from a very superior force, he remained at his post, keeping his ship HM Drifter "Coral Haven", heading for the enemy, and encouraging his crew to fight their small gun. Four rounds were fired, and he and his crew only escaped from their ship when she was on fire and in a sinking condition.
- Skipper Dennis John Nichols, RNR 834 WSA.
  He remained at his post in the wheel house, steering his ship, HM Drifter Floandi, and although wounded himself, assisted in

removing the more severely wounded members of his crew. Later he went in a small boat, plugging the holes in ship's side, thereby enabling her to reach port.
To receive a Bar to the Distinguished Service Cross.
- Lieut. Robert Henry Baunton, DSC, RNR
  He was in charge of the patrol line, and did extremely good work in rallying the Drifters and reorganising the various groups.

The KING has been graciously pleased to approve of the award of the Distinguished Service Cross for services in action with enemy submarines:—
LG 29.8.1917 p 8987

- Lieut. Frederick Albert Richardson, RN
- Lieut. George Spencer, RNR
- Lieut. Henry Joseph Osborne, RNR
- Lieut. Evans Stanley MacLennan, RNR
- Lieut. Adam Yule Catto, RNR
- Sub. Lieut. George Hambrook Dean Doubleday, RNR
- Sub. Lieut. Charles Murray Mutch, RNVR
- Gnr. (T) Thomas Alfred Browning, RN
- Skipper William Smith, RNR 1683 SA
- Skipper Richard Webb Hannaford, RNR 1389 SA
- Skipper William Moodie, RNR 2140 WSA
- Skipper Arthur Bland, RNR 622 WSA

To receive a Bar to the Distinguished Service Cross:—
- Lieut. William Strickland Harrison, DSC, RNR
- Sub. Lieut. Keith Morris, DSC, RNR

The following Awards of the Distinguished Service Cross have been approved:—
LG 29.8.1917 p 8988.

- Flt. Lieut. Henry McClelland, RNAS
- Lieut. Percy Townley Rawlings, RNVR
  In recognition of their services on the night of the 9th July 1917, when a successful attack was carried out against the Turkish-German fleet lying off Constantinople.
  When the "Goeben", surrounded by warships (including submarines) had been located, the attack was made from a height of 800 feet. Direct hits were obtained on the Goeben and on the other enemy ships near her. Big explosions took place on board them, followed by a heavy conflagration.
  The War Office at Constantinople was also attacked and a direct hit obtained.
- Flt. Sub. Lieut. Lacey Norman Glaisby, RNAS
  In recognition of his services on the 20th July 1917, during a bombing raid on Aertrycke

aerodrome. He was attacked by a hostile machine whilst over the target, and fought an engagement lasting twenty minutes. Flt. Sub. Lieut. Glaisby was wounded in the head, and his observer was shot through the arm shortly after the engagement began, but they succeeded in driving the enemy machine down in a vertical nose dive.

- Flt. Sub. Lieut. (act. Flt. Lieut) Alfred Williams Carter, RNAS
  This officer has at all times led his patrols with great courage, skill and pertinacity, often engaging superior numbers of hostile aircraft. On the 22nd July 1917, he engaged single handed for half an hour five enemy scouts which he prevented from carrying out a reconnaissance.
  On the 24th July 1917, with one other pilot he attacked four enemy aircraft, one of which he drove down completely out of control.
- Flt. Lieut. Lancelot Giberne Sieveking, RNAS
- Flt. Sub. Lieut. John Roy Allan, RNAS.
  In recognition of their services in dropping bombs on enemy railway lines and ammunition dumps on the night of the 11th-12th July 1917.
- Obsr. Lieut. Ronald George St. John, RNAS
  In recognition of his services on the 20th July 1917, during a bombing raid on Aertrycke aerodrome. After the bombs had been dropped on the objective, his machine was attacked by an Albatross Scout, which he shot down at point blank range. Another hostile machine then attacked, but was driven off.

To receive a Bar to the Distinguished Service Cross.
- Flt. Cdr. Thomas Frederick Le Mesurier, DSC, RNAS
  For consistent skill and courage in leading his flight on bombing raids, particularly on the 28th July 1917.

The KING has been graciously pleased to approve of the award of the Distinguished Service Cross:—
LG 29.8.1917 p 8988

- Lieut. Illtyd Dillwyn Llewellyn, RNR

The KING has been graciously pleased to approve of the award of the Distinguished Service Cross to the undermentioned Officers of the British Mercantile Marine, in recognition of zeal and devotion to duty shown in carrying on the trade of the country during the war:—
LG 29.8.1917 p 8989

- Capt. Daniel Evans
- Capt. John MacMillan
- Capt. Crawford George Smith
- Capt. William Thomas King
- Ch. Engr. Edward Gordon

The following Awards of the Distinguished Service Cross have been approved:—
LG 14.9.1917 p 9535

- Lieut. George Haines Faulkner, RN
- Lieut. Edmund Gerald Noel Rushbrooke, RN
- Payr. Kenneth Edgar Badcock RN
- Gnr. (T) John Henry Evans, RN
  For their services in vessels of the Harwich Force during the war.

The KING has been graciously pleased to approve of the award of the Distinguished Service Cross to Officers for services in action with enemy Submarines:—
LG 14.9.1917 p 9536

- Flt. Lieut. (actg. Flt. Cdr) Osborne Arthur Butcher, RNAS
- Flt. Lieut. John Osborn Galpin, RNAS
- Lieut. John Henry Blyth, RNR
- Flt. Sub. Lieut. Charles Leslie Young, RNAS
- Skipper Albert Lawrence Petherbridge, RNR
- Skipper Alexander McLeod, RNR 2137 WSA

To receive a Bar to the Distinguished Service Cross.
- Flt. Lieut. Warren Rawson Mackenzie, DSC, RNAS

The following Awards of the Distinguished Service Cross have been approved:—
LG 14.9.1917 p 9537

- Flt. Lieut. (Act Flt. Cdr) Robert Jope Slade,. RNAS
  For his services during a bombing raid on Snelleghem Aerodrome on the 5th August 1917.
  He was attacked by an enemy machine when leaving the target. After firing about thirty rounds, the hostile machine appeared to lose control and suddenly dived without regaining it.
- Flt. Lieut. (Act. Flt. Cdr) William Melville Alexander, RNAS
  On 16th August 1917, he attacked at about 3,000 feet two hostile scouts, one of which, after a short combat, fell completely out of control.
  On 20th August 1917, while returning from patrol, he observed three enemy scouts. These he pursued until they turned to fight. One of the scouts he shot down completely out of control, and the remaining two dived away.

On 21st August 1917, while on an offensive patrol he attacked and drove down completely out of control an enemy scout which was attacking another member of his patrol.

Flt. Lieut. Alexander has at all times shown the greatest bravery and determination.

- Flt Sub. Lieut. Charles Philip Oldfield Bartlett, RNAS.

For exceptionally good work on the occasion of a bombing raid on Houttave Aerodrome on the 25th July 1917.

To receive a Bar to the Distinguished Service Cross.

- Flt. Cdr. Irwin Napier Colin Clarke, DSC, RNAS.

For exceptionally good work on the occasion of a bombing raid on Houttave Aerodrome on the 25th July 1917.

This officer has shown great skill and persistence in leading his flight on many occasions.

The KING has been graciously pleased to approve of the award of the Distinguished Service Cross to the undermentioned Officers of the British Mercantile Marine, in recognition of zeal and devotion to duty shown in carrying on the trade of the country during the war. *LG 14.9.1917 p 9537*

- Capt. Charles Ruthven Stewart,
- Capt. Edward John Holl

The KING has been graciously pleased to give orders for the award of the Distinguished Service Cross to the undermentioned Officers in recognition of their services as mentioned in the foregoing despatch. (The Tigris, December 1916 to March 1917, *LG 21.9.1917 pp 9819/22*) *LG 21.9.1917 p 9823*

- Lieut. R. P. D. Webster, RN, HMS "Snakefly".

Has shown judgement and resource on many occasions under fire.

- Lieut. J. P. Bradley, RNR, HMS "Firefly".

For coolness under fire on all occasions. Lieut. Bradley did very good work by personally taking the captured Turkish steamer "Basra" down the river laden with enemy wounded.

- Lieut. Hugh Lincoln, RNR, HMS "Flycatcher".

For good work while in command of HM ships "Comet" and "Flycatcher", and he has carried out the duty of forward observing Officer under fire in a very satisfactory manner.

- Lieut. John H. A. Wood, MC, RNVR, HMS "Moth".

Who was severely wounded while firing a machine-gun in a totally exposed position.

- Sub. Lieut. E. C. W. Vane Tempest, RNVR, HMS "Mantis".

Was in charge of the gunnery of the ship, and while under hot fire he did his duty with coolness. At one time he personally worked a maxim though wounded.

- Sub. Lieut. G. A. Feilman, RNVR, HMS "Tarantula".

For coolness and resource under very heavy fire, in firing with machine-guns on the Turkish infantry and machine-guns, when all other men were employed in working the main armaments of 6 in., 12 pdr. and pom-poms.

- Surgeon J. C. Kelly, RN, HMS "Tarantula".

Attended to wounded whilst fire was at its hottest in an exposed position.

- Surgeon James P. Shorten, RN, HMS "Mantis".

Continued to dress and attend to the wounded in the open while under very heavy fire.

- Temporary Surgeon Robert G. Elwell, RN, HMS "Gadfly".

Has rendered valuable service under fire on many occasions.

The KING has been graciously pleased to give orders for the award of the Distinguished Service Cross to the undermentioned Officers:—
LG 1.10.1917 pp 10153/4

- Lieut. Jocelyn Heneage Drummond, RN
- Lieut. Arthur Rowland Banks, RN
- Lieut. Neville Duncan Burleigh Taylor, RN
- Lieut. John Cracroft Amcotts, RN
- Payr. Roger Ernest Worthington, RN
- Lieut. William Avern, RNR
- Lieut. Claude Bennett Walker, RNR
- Lieut. William Birtles, RNR
- Engr. Lieut. William Peterson, RNR
- Actg. Lieut. John Henderson Jack, RNR
- Actg. Lieut. Charles Thomas Wilson, RNR
- Ch. Gnr. John Steel, RN
- Ch. Gnr. Leonard Parsons, RN
- Gnr. (T) Alexander George Stock, RN
- Gnr (T) Albert William Grose, RN

To receive a Bar to the Distinguished Service Cross:—
- Lieut. Rodolph Henry Fane De Salis, DSC, RN

The KING has been graciously pleased to approve of the award of the Distinguished Service Cross to Officers of the Royal Naval Air Service:—

(1) For services on patrol duties and submarine searching in Home Waters:—
LG 1.10.1917 p 10155

- Flt. Cdr. George Fred Breese, RNAS
- Flt. Cdr. Arthur Quilton Cooper, RNAS
- Flt. Cdr. John Sylvester Wheelwright, RNAS
- Flt. Cdr. James Gardner Struthers, RNAS
- Flt. Cdr. Clarence MacLaurin, RNAS
- Flt. Lieut. John Anthony Carr, RNAS
- Flt. Lieut. Frederic William Walker, RNAS
- Flt. Lieut. Charles Sydney Coltson,
- Flt. Lieut. John Francis Dixon, RNAS
- Flt. Lieut. Arthur Stanley Elliott, RNAS
- Flt. Sub. Lieut. Thomas Godfrey Currie Wood, RNAS
- Flt. Sub. Lieut. William Jerome de Salis, RNAS
- Flt. Sub. Lieut. Arthur Leslie Simms, RNAS
- Flt. Sub. Lieut. Harold Marsh Morris, RNAS

To receive a Bar to the Distinguished Service Cross.
- Sqdrn. Cdr. Frederick Joseph Rutland, DSC, RNAS

(2) For services in reconnaissance and bombing flights in the Eastern Mediterranean:—
LG 1.10.1917 p 10156

- Sqdrn. Cdr. Herbert Stanley Adams, RNAS

The KING has been graciously pleased to approve of the award of the Distinguished Service Cross to officers for services in action with enemy submarines.
LG 2.11.1917 pp 11315/6

- Flt. Lieut. Thomas Henry Newton, RNAS
- Act. Lieut. James Jickell, RNR
- Act. Lieut. Walter Henry Frame, RNR
- Surg. Prob. Alexander Coutts Fowler, RNVR
- Skipper Henry Newman, RNR
- Ch. Gnr. James Hamilton, RN
- Warrt. Teleg. Allan Andrews, RNR

To Receive a Bar to the Distinguished Service Cross.
- Engr. Lieut. (Act. Engr. Lieut. Cdr) Leonard Samuel Loveless, DSO, DSC, RNR
- Lieut. Ronald James Mortimer, DSC, RNR
- Lieut. John Lawrie, DSO, DSC, RNR
- Lieut. Thomas Hughes, DSC, RNR
- Engr. Lieut. James William Grant, DSC, RNR
- Act. Lieut. Francis Robert Hereford, DSO, DSC, RNR

To Receive a Second Bar to the Distinguished Service Cross.
- Lieut. Stephen Philip Robey White, DSC, RNR
- Staff. Payr. William Richard Ashton, DSC, RN

The KING has been graciously pleased to approve of the award of the Distinguished Service Cross to the undermentioned officers in recognition of their services in submarines in enemy waters:—
LG 2.11.1917 p 11317

- Lieut. Cromwell Hanford Varley, RN
- Lieut. Alan Courtenay Moncrieff Bennett, RN
- Lieut. George John Mackness, RN
- Lieut. Clive Askew Robinson, RN
- Lieut. John Jasper Ray Peirson, RN
- Lieut. John Maurice Mansfield, RN
- Lieut. Thomas Arthur Watterson, RNR
- Lieut. John Hamilton Blair, RNR
- Art. Engr. William James Williams, RN
- Art. Eng. Harold Lindsay Smith, RN

To receive a Bar to the Distinguished Service Cross.
- Lieut. Charles Manners Sutton Chapman, DSC, RN

The KING has been graciously pleased to approve of the award of the Distinguished Service Cross to the undermentioned officers:—

- Lieut. Eric Pole Welman, RN
  In recognition of his gallantry in action off the Belgian Coast.
- Lieut. Alpin Errol Thomson, RN
- Sub. Lieut. Robert Cuming, RNVR
  In recognition of their gallantry when one of HM minesweepers struck a mine.

To receive a Bar to the Distinguished Service Cross.
- Lieut. Alexander Daniells, DSC, RNR.
- Act. Lieut. Henry Beattie Bell-Irving, DSC, RNVR
  In recognition of their gallantry when one of HM minesweepers struck a mine.

The KING has been graciously pleased to approve of the award of the Distinguished Service Cross to officers of the Royal Naval Air Service:—
LG 2.11.1917 pp 11320/1

- Flt. Cdr. Harold Austen Buss, RNAS
  For his services on the occasion of a bombing raid on Bruges Docks on the night of the 2nd/3rd September 1917, when numerous direct hits on the docks, submarine shelters and railway sidings on the quay were obtained.
- Act. Flt. Cdr. Stearne Tighe Edwards, RNAS
  In recognition of his services on the following occasions:—
  On the 3rd September 1917, with his flight he attacked a two seater Aviatik. The enemy

machine was observed to go down in a vertical nose dive, and the enemy observer was seen to collapse in the cockpit.

On the 21st September 1917, he drove a two seater enemy machine down out of control.

On the 23rd September 1917 he attacked an Albatross scout, which crashed into the sea.

On the same date he attacked three Albatross scouts. One got on the tail of another officer's machine at very close range, shooting him up very badly. Flt. Cdr. Edwards attacked him from above, and the enemy machine turned on its back and went down in a vertical dive. He followed the enemy machine down to 8,000 feet, when its wings came off and it fell to the ground.

- Act. Flt. Cdr. Howard John Thomas Saint, RNAS.

For conspicuous bravery in attacking superior hostile formations of enemy aircraft.

On the 21st September 1917, he, with three other machines, attacked five hostile scouts. After getting to close quarters with one of them, he fired three bursts from his machine-gun and drove it down completely out of control.

On the 23rd September 1917, while leading a patrol of eight scouts, he attacked a hostile formation of ten machines. One of these he drove down, diving vertically out of control. He has forced down other machines completely out of control, one of them in flames, and has also shown great courage in attacking enemy troops and aerodromes with machine-gun fire from very low altitudes.

- Flt. Lieut. Harold Spencer Kerby, RNAS

For the great courage and initiative shown by him on many occasions, notably on the 12th August 1917, when he attacked hostile machines returning from a raid on England. One hostile machine was driven down by him to the water, where it was observed to turn over.

- Flt. Lieut. John Fleming Jones, RNAS.

In recognition of his services on the night of the 15th-16th August 1917, when under adverse weather conditions, he dropped bombs on railway sidings at Ostend, causing a fire which continued to burn as long as it was under observation.

- Flt. Lieut. Arthur Frank Brandon, RNAS (since killed).

For services on the 22nd August 1917, when he attacked single handed an enemy formation returning from a raid on England and brought down one of them in flames. As his aeroplane had been hit several times, he landed to

change machines, and proceeded to attack again with a new one, making repeated attacks on individual machines, and pursuing the enemy formation over the North Sea to the Belgian coast, where he made a final attack.

- Flt. Lieut. Ronald Roscoe Thornley, RNAS.

For gallantry and skill in aerial combats, notably on the following occasions:—

On the 16th June 1917, whilst on patrol, he attacked a two seater Aviatik, which fell to the ground, inside our lines.

On the 15th August 1917, he attacked an Albatross scout and shot it down out of control.

On the 19th August 1917, he attacked an Aviatik and drove it down out of control.

On the 11th September 1917, he engaged one of three enemy machines, firing about fifty rounds when quite close, apparently wounding the observer at once, and shortly afterwards the enemy machine fell out of control.

- Act. Flt. Lieut. Richard Pearman Minifie, RNAS.

In recognition of his services on the following occasions:

On the 22nd April 1917 he destroyed two enemy scouts.

On the 8th August 1917 he brought down an Albatross scout in flames.

On the 16th September 1917, he destroyed an Albatross scout. On the 19th September 1917, he crashed an Albatross scout.

In addition to the above mentioned combats, he has driven down numerous enemy machines out of control, and on the 3rd July, 1917, he attacked parties of troops on the road from a height of 200 feet.

On the 19th August 1917, he attacked two enemy aerodromes, firing 450 rounds at the hangars from a height of 400 feet.

On the 20th September 1917, he did excellent work in detecting and scattering troops massing for counter attacks, flying at an extremely low altitude.

- Act. Flt. Lieut. (now Flt. Lieut) Arthur Roy Brown, RNAS

For the excellent work he has done on active service.

On the 3rd September 1917 he attacked a two seater Aviatik in company with his flight. The enemy machine was seen to dive down vertically, the enemy observer falling over on the side of the fuselage shot.

On the 5th September 1917, in company with formation, he attacked an Albatross scout and two seater, driving them away from our lines. One machine was observed to go down apparently out of control.

On the 15th September 1917, whilst on patrol, he dived on two Aviatiks, and three Albatross scouts, followed by his flight. He dived several times and picked out one enemy scout, firing about 200 rounds, when the enemy machine went down out of control, spinning on its back.

On the 20th September 1917, whilst leading his flight, he dived on five Albatross Scouts. Flt. Lieut. Brown picked out one enemy machine and opened fire. One of his guns jammed, but he carried on with the other. The enemy machine went down out of control and over on its back, and remained in that position for about thirty seconds, whilst Flt. Lieut. Brown continued firing until his other gun jammed. The enemy machine then disappeared in the clouds, still on its back.

Another officer of the same patrol was later followed by four enemy machines, as he was separated from the formation. Both Flt. Lieut. Brown's guns were jammed, but he dived on the enemy machines and drove them off, thus undoubtedly saving the pilot's life.

- Act. Flt. Lieut. (now Flt. Lieut). Desmond Fitzgerald Fitzgibbon, RNAS
For exceptional courage and determination in leading offensive patrols against enemy formations, although often outnumbered by them. On the 14th September 1917, he and his patrol of seven machines attacked a hostile formation of eight enemy scouts. In the combat that ensued, three hostile machines were brought down completely out of control, one of these by Flt. Lieut. Fitzgibbon, while the patrol suffered no casualties.
On the 26th September 1917, he attacked with his patrol of eight machines fifteen hostile scouts. He himself engaged four different machines, one after the other, finally driving one down completely out of control.
- Flt. Sub. Lieut. Charles Beverley Sproatt, RNAS
Carried out a bombing attack on Bruges Docks on the 4th September 1917, obtaining direct hits. He was subjected to heavy and accurate anti-aircraft fire, and his machine was shot about and radiator pierced.
- Flt. Sub. Lieut. Leonard William Ormerod, RNAS
- Flt. Sub. Lieut. John Southey Wright, RNAS
In recognition of their services on the 5th September 1917, when they carried out a bombing attack on Bruges Docks, obtaining direct hits.
- Flt. Sub. Lieut. William Allan Scott, RNAS.
In recognition of his services on the night of the 15th-16th August 1917, when in spite of difficult conditions, he dropped bombs on Thourout railway station and sidings. He circled the objective for an hour at a height of 3,000 feet, dropping his bombs singly, and achieved good results.
- Obsr. Sub. Lieut. Paul Brewsher, RNAS.
In recognition of his services on the night of the 15th-16th August 1917, when, with Flt. Lieut. Jones, in spite of adverse weather conditions, he dropped bombs on railway sidings at Ostend, causing a fire which continued to burn as long as it was under observation.

The KING has been graciously pleased to approve of the award of the the Distinguished Service Cross to the undermentioned Officers of the British Mercantile Marine, in recognition of zeal and devotion to duty shown in carrying on the trade of the country during the war:—
LG 2.11.1917 p 11321

- Capt. Henry Saunders
- Capt. Henry George Speed
- Capt. William Philip Hains

The KING has been graciously pleased to approve of the award of the Distinguished Service Cross to officers for services in action with enemy submarines:—
LG 17.11.1917 p 11921

- Lieut. (now Lieut. Cdr.) Kenneth Michell, RN
- Lieut. Charles Stuart Burgon, RNR
- Lieut. Nicholas Frederick Smiles, RNR
- Lieut. Alexander MacRae, RNR
- Engr. Lieut. William Begg McDonald, RNR (since killed)
- Act. Lieut. Claude Martin Butlin, RN
- Act. Lieut. Lancelot Vivian Donne, RN
- Act. Lieut. Arthur John Booth, RNR
- Act. Lieut. Joseph Russell Stenhouse, RNR
- Flt. Sub. Lieut. Charles Stanley Mossop, RNAS
- Asst. Payr. Harry Manley, RNR
- Act. Sub. Lieut. Benjamin Evans, RNR
- Act. Sub. Lieut. George Edmunds Martin, RNR
- Gnr. (T) Samuel Baker, RN
- Skpr. James Ballard, RNR 1099 WSA
- Skpr. Alexander Forbes, RNR 175 SA
- Skpr. Samuel Charles Kennington, RNR (FR)
- Skpr. John Watson, RNR 318 WSA
- Skpr. Frederick William White, RNR, 72 SA

To receive a Bar to the Distinguished Service Cross:—
- Sub. Lieut. Reginald Allen, DSC, RNR

The KING has been graciously pleased to approve of the award of the Distinguished Service Cross to Officers of the Royal Naval Air Service:—
LG 17.11.1917 p 11923

- Flt. Cdr. Gerald Essex Hervey, RNAS
For conspicuous gallantry and devotion to duty in air fights and bombing raids. On the 22nd August 1917, he attacked a formation of ten hostile aircraft engaged in a raid on England and brought one of them down into the sea.
- Act. Flt. Cdr. Henry Guy Holden, RNAS
In recognition of the great courage and gallantry displayed by him in obtaining important photographs under heavy anti-aircraft fire on the 14th October 1917, and on other occasions. He has also on many occasions been the pilot of spotting machines.
- Flt. Sub. Lieut. (now Flt. Lieut) Victor Richard Gibbs, RNAS
For conspicuous gallantry and devotion to duty in numerous night bombing raids, particularly on the night of the 25th September 1917, when in spite of difficult weather conditions he carried out a double trip and made good shooting from 3,000 feet and below, and was responsible for dropping over $1^1/_2$ tons of bombs on his objectives.
- Flt. Sub. Lieut. (now Flt. Lieut) Leonard Horatio Slatter, RNAS
For conspicuous gallantry and skill on many occasions both as observer and pilot. He has taken part in numerous night bombing raids, and on one occasion he ascended at night for the purpose of attacking hostile machines, notwithstanding the fact that he had only returned a few hours previously from a successful action with hostile aircraft in superior numbers.
On the 4th September 1917, he attacked an enemy Torpedo Boat Destroyer with machine-gun fire.
- Flt. Sub. Lieut. Stanley Wallace Rosevear, RNAS
For conspicuous gallantry and devotion to duty. He has destroyed several hostile machines, and has also attacked and scattered parties of enemy infantry from low altitudes, on one occasion from a height of only 100 feet.
- Flt. Sub. Lieut. Frederic Ross Johnson, RNAS.
For conspicuous gallantry and devotion to duty in a bombing raid on Thourout Railway Station on the night of the 20th-21st September 1917, when he came down to about 3,000 feet and made particularly good shooting

The KING has been graciously pleased to approve of the award of the Distinguished Service Cross to the undermentioned Officers of the British Mercantile Marine, in recognition of zeal and devotion to duty shown in carrying on the trade of the country during the war:—
LG 17.11.1917 p 11923

- Capt. Rowland Robinson Barker
- Capt. Frederic Hadley Bryant
- Capt. Samuel Cook
- Capt. Henry John
- Capt. Walter Keslake
- Capt. James Lee
- Capt. Neil McNeill
- Capt. William Surman Mason
- Capt. Joseph Stephen Meria
- Capt. George Moir
- Capt. David Russell Murray
- Capt. Richard Edward Oliver
- Capt. Henry George Orchard
- Capt. Edwin Alan Porter
- Capt. Isaac Bedlington Tose
- Capt. Peter Urquhart
- Capt. Edward Witten
- Ch. Offr. William Whitehead
- Ch. Engr. Oliver Henry Jelley

To receive a Bar to the Distinguished Service Cross.
- Capt. Rowland Robinson Barker, DSC

The KING has been graciously pleased to approve of the award of the Distinguished Service Cross to Officers for services in action with enemy submarines:—
LG 30.11.1917 p.12547

To receive a Bar to the Distinguished Service Cross.
- Flt. Lieut. Basil Deacon Hobbs, DSO, DSC, RNAS

To receive a Second bar to the Distinguished Service Cross
- Flt. Sub. Lieut. (now Flt. Lieut) Frederick Lea Dickey, DSC, RNAS

The KING has been graciously pleased to approve of the award of the Distinguished Service Cross to the undermentioned Officers:—
LG 30.11.1917 pp 12547/8

- Lieut. Thomas Benbow McNabb, RNVR
In recognition of his gallantry in going overboard and securing a line to a drifting mine after attempts to sink it by gunfire had failed owing to a choppy sea and considerable swell which made accurate shooting impossible.
- Lieut. Samuel Jackson Hanna, RNVR

In recognition of his services with a Naval armoured car squadron in Belgium, France, the Dobrudja and Galicia. He has carried out his duties as Assistant Adjutant and Adjutant with conspicuous success and always shown himself to be a plucky and unselfish officer.
- Lieut. George Reginald Turner, RNVR
In recognition of his services with a Naval armoured car squadron in Galicia. In the trenches opposite Brzezany he beat back the German attack with his maxim parties. He was struck by a shell but refused to leave his post for 48 hours until off his head from the shock.
- Lieut. John Andrew Quarrie, RNR
In recognition of his services in submarines.

The KING has been graciously pleased to approve of the award of the Distinguished Service Cross to Officers of the Royal Naval Air Service:—
LG 30.11.1917 pp 12548/9

- Act. Flt. Cdr. Fred Carr Armstrong, RNAS
In recognition of his services with a Wing of the RNAS at Dunkirk between February and September 1917. He has destroyed several hostile machines, and has led his flight with very great skill and gallantry.
- Flt. Lieut. Harold Francis Beamish, RNAS
In recognition of his services with a Wing of the RNAS at Dunkirk between January and September 1917, during which time he has destroyed several hostile machines and driven down numerous others.
- Flt. Sub. Lieut. (now Flt. Lieut) Edwin Tufnell Hayne, RNAS.
In recognition of his services with a Wing of the RNAS at Dunkirk between March and September 1917. He has had numerous engagements with enemy aircraft, and on the 16th August 1917, attacked an enemy aerodrome and placed a whole flight of machines out of action by machine-gun fire. During a flight of over two hours, during which time he attacked transport and railways, he never exceeded a height of 1,000 feet.
- Flt. Sub. Lieut. Geoffrey William Hemming, RNAS
In recognition of his services with a Wing of the RNAS at Dunkirk between March and September 1917, during which period he has been continuously employed on the Belgian coast, and on many occasions has been in charge of a flight. On the 22nd September 1917, he led his flight against a formation of twenty enemy aircraft, and engaging three consecutively, brought them all down.

- Flt. Sub. Lieut. John Ellis Langford Hunter, RNAS
In recognition of his services with a Wing of the RNAS at Dunkirk between July and September 1917, during which time he has carried out continuous work on offensive patrols. On the 22nd September 1917, he destroyed two enemy aircraft which were attempting to interfere with our spotting machines.

To receive a Bar to the Distinguished Service Cross.
- Act. Flt. Cdr. Richard Pearman Minifie, DSC, RNAS
For conspicuous gallantry in air fighting throughout October 1917, during which period he has destroyed several enemy machines and driven down others out of control.

The KING has been graciously pleased to approve of the award of the Distinguished Service Cross to the undermentioned officers of the British Mercantile Marine, in recognition of zeal and devotion to duty shown in carrying on the trade of the country during the war:—
LG 30.11.1917 p 12549

- Capt. Thomas Henry Beard
- Capt. Joseph Brown
- Capt. Theobald John Claude Buret
- Capt. John Crockart
- Capt. George Fenby Hiles
- Capt. David Isaac Jenkins
- Capt. James Herbert Needler (since died)
- Capt. William Park Purdon
- Capt. Edward Wilson Rettie
- Capt. Francis Thomas Skellern

The KING has been graciously pleased to approve of the award of the Distinguished Service Cross to Officers and Men for services in action with enemy submarines.
LG 19.12.1917 p 13317

- Lieut. Henry Neville Lake, RN
- Lieut. George Gillen Asbury, RNR
- Flt. Sub. Lieut. (now Flt. Lieut) Norman Ansley Magor, RNAS
- Act. Lieut. Eric Templer Wiggins, RN
- Flt. Sub. Lieut. Ronald Jarman, RNAS
- Ch. Gnr. Thomas Frederick Britton, RN
- Gnr. Henry Samuel Randall, RN

To receive a Bar to the Distinguished Service Cross.
- Lieut. Alexander MacRae, DSC, RN
- Flt. Lieut. Ernest John Cuckney, DSC, RNAS

To receive a Second Bar to the Distinguished Service Cross.

- Flt. Cdr. Theodore Douglas Hallam, DSC, RNAS

The KING has been graciously pleased to approve of the award of the Distinguished Service Cross to Officers of the Royal Naval Air Service:—
LG 19.12.1917 p 13318

- Flt. Lieut. Richard Gregory Gardner, RNAS
  In recognition of the great zeal and gallantry displayed by him on the night of the 15th October 1917, when a bombing raid was carried out on Bruges Docks and good results obtained in spite of heavy and accurate anti-aircraft fire. This officer has taken part in thirty-six bombing raids.
- Flt. Lieut. John William Alcock, RNAS (now prisoner)
  For the great skill, judgement and dash displayed by him off Mudros on the 30th September 1917, in a successful attack on three enemy seaplanes, two of which were brought down in the sea.
- Flt. Sub. Lieut. (now Flt. Lieut) Charles Ferris Montagu Chambers, RNAS
  During the combined naval and military operations in the neighbourhood of Lindi, East Africa, on the 10th and 11th June, 1917, this officer flew his machine at all hours of the day under heavy fire with excellent results, bringing back to his Commanding Officer clear and concise reports.
- Flt. Sub. Lieut. (act. Flt. Lieut.) Wilfred Austin Curtis, RNAS
  For conspicuous gallantry and devotion to duty. He has on many occasions destroyed and driven down out of control enemy machines. On the 21st October 1917, in a combined attack with two other pilots, he sent down an enemy machine in flames, and twenty minutes later he followed another enemy scout from 10,000 to 2,000 feet, and sent it down in a vertical dive, which ended in a crash.
- Obs. Lieut. Cyril Chapman, RNAS
  In recognition of the great gallantry and skill displayed by him on the 18th October 1917, when he carried out a photographic reconnaissance in spite of adverse conditions and intense cold, as a result of which he was severely frostbitten. He has repeatedly carried out valuable photographic reconnaissances at long distances behind the enemy lines under very heavy and extremely accurate anti-aircraft fire and despite the tactics of enemy aircraft.
- Flt. Sub. Lieut. Charles Roger Lupton, RNAS
- Flt. Sub. Lieut. Euan Dickson, RNAS

- Obs. Sub. Lieut. William Laurence Hill Pattisson, RNAS
  For conspicuous gallantry and devotion to duty in a bombing raid on Thourout Railway Station and Varsennaere Aerodrome on the 25th October 1917. These officers volunteered for the expedition in spite of extremely unfavourable weather conditions. They have all previously taken part in many bombing raids.
- Flt. Sub. Lieut. John Gerald Manuel, RNAS
  For conspicuous gallantry and devotion to duty in air fights and bombing raids, particularly on the 26th September 1917, when he attacked alone the Abeele Aerodrome, dropping his bombs from about 1,500 feet with good results. A machine-gun then opened fire on him but he dived down low and silenced it by firing fifty rounds from his machine-gun.
- Obs. Sub. Lieut. Thomas Terrell, RNAS
  For conspicuous gallantry and devotion to duty in a long distance bombing raid on the 28th October 1917, when a direct hit was obtained on a munitions factory. He was heavily attacked by machine-gun fire on his homeward journey which was carried out under exceedingly trying conditions. He has also carried out other bombing raids and a number of photographic reconnaissances.

To receive a Bar to the Distinguished Service Cross.

- Flt. Lieut. (act Flt. Cdr) Joseph Stewart Temple Fall, DSC, RNAS.
  In recognition of the conspicuous courage displayed by him in attacking enemy aircraft in superior numbers on many occasions. On the 15th October 1917, he attacked an enemy machine from in front at very close range, at times within twenty five yards. He then turned sharply and attacked from behind, sending the enemy machine down spinning on its back and emitting great volumes of black smoke.
- Flt. Lieut. Harold Thomas Mellings, DSC, RNAS.
  For the great skill, judgement and dash displayed by him off Mudros on the 30th September 1917, in a successful attack on three enemy seaplanes, two of which were brought down in the sea.

To receive a Second Bar to the Distinguished Service Cross.

- Flt. Lieut. (act. Flt. Cdr) Joseph Stewart Temple Fall, DSC, RNAS.
  In recognition of his services on the 12th and 13th November 1917, when he had successful engagements with three enemy machines. He has always shown great courage and gallantry in the face of the enemy, and maintained a

high record of achievement, having destroyed many enemy machines.

The KING has been graciously pleased to approve of the award of the Distinguished Service Cross to the undermentioned Officer:—
LG 19.12.1917 p 13319

- Gnr. Mark Methuen, RN
During the combined naval and military operations in the neighbourhood of Lindi, East Africa, on the 10th and 11th June, 1917, the ship in which Mr. Methuen was serving was hit by an enemy 4.1 shell. Hearing that a fire had been started, he immediately proceeded aft and descended to the after flat, which was full of fumes and smoke, to investigate the course of the fire and to take the necessary steps to extinguish it. Whilst carrying out this task he was exposed to the effects of the shell gas, as a result of which he had to be placed on the sick list. His coolness and judgement prevented the fire from spreading.

The KING has been graciously pleased to approve of the award of the Distinguished Service Cross to the undermentioned Officers of the British Mercantile Marine, in recognition of zeal and devotion to duty shown in carrying on the trade of the country during the War:—
LG 19.12.1917 p 13319

- Capt. John Begg
- Capt. Robert Logan
- Capt. John Martin Parker
- Capt. Thomas Strike
- Capt. Charles Vermulen
- Ch. Offr. Alfred Henderson Moodie
- 2nd Engr. James Laws Pennington

The KING has been graciously pleased to approve of the award of the Distinguished Service Cross for services in action with enemy submarines:—
LG 22.2.1918 pp 2301/2

- Flt. Lieut. James Frederick Hart, RNAS
- Flt. Lieut. John Eld Barrs, RNAS
- Lieut. Douglas Ramsden Attwood, RNR
- Lieut. Harold Luke Forster, RNR
- Lieut. Norman Leslie, RNR
- Lieut. John Isdale, RNR
- Lieut. Francis Graham John Manning, RNR
- Engr. Lieut. Neil Shaw MacKinnon, RNR (since killed)
- Lieut. John Francis Buller Kitson, RNVR
- Lieut. Alexander John Mackenzie, RNVR
- Act. Lieut. Ernest Hutchison, RNR
- Sub. Lieut. Murdo Murchison, RNR

- Gnr. James Barber Gledhill, RN
- Art. Engr. Herbert Robbins, RN
- Mid. Frederick William Hartley, RNR
- Skpr. Richard William Barker, RNR 725 WSA
- Skpr. James Culling, RNR 380 WSA
- Skpr. Edward Hemp, RNR 726 WSA
- Skpr. Thomas Lane, RNR 220 WSA

To receive a Bar to the Distinguished Service Cross.
- Flt. Cdr. James Gardner Struthers, DSC, RNAS

To receive a Second Bar to the Distinguished Service Cross.
- Flt. Cdr. James Gardner Struthers, DSC, RNAS

The KING has been graciously pleased to approve of the award of the Distinguished Service Cross to the undermentioned Officers:—
LG 22.2.1918 p 2303

- Surgn. Alexander Frederick Richmond Wollaston, M.B., M.A., RN.
For conspicuous devotion to duty and for his unfailing care of the sick and wounded during military operations in East Africa.
During the operations in the Rufigi River Delta he voluntarily attended to the casualties of the Rufigi River transport service in addition to those of his own unit.
- Capt. Walter George Arthur Shadwell, RMA
For the courageous manner in which he behaved on the 28th November 1915. His prompt action and judgement saved his gun and he was responsible for the removal of the wounded to safety, and for getting his gun and stores away so that they were able to bring them into action the following day.
His conduct on this and other occasions showed the highest qualities of an officer.
- Lieut. John Samuel James, RNR.
- Skpr. Francis Joint Hulland, RNR, 1522 SA
In recognition of their services in minesweeping operations abroad during the period June 1916, to June 1917.
- Lieut. James Pittendrigh, RNR
In recognition of gallant conduct and good seamanship under fire. Whilst he was on patrol in HM Trawler Restrivo in the Kos Channel, on the 25th October 1917, fire was opened on him from the shore. At the same time a caique, flying the Italian flag, was seen between the trawler and the shore, dismasted and drifting towards the enemy coast. Though a strong southerly wind was blowing and the sea was rough, Lieut. Pittendrigh closed the caique, took her in tow, and brought her into safety. The enemy meantime maintained a hot fire

from a 4 inch gun, to which the trawler, owing to her inferior armament, was unable to make an effective reply.

The KING has been graciously pleased to approve of the award of the Distinguished Service Cross to officers of the Royal Naval Air Service:—
LG 28.2.1918 pp 2304/5

- Flt. Cdr. Wilfred Henry Dunn, RNAS.
  In recognition of his services whilst employed in connection with military operations in East Africa. He did splendid work during the operations in the Lindi area, and carried out valuable bombing and reconnaissance flights.
- Flt. Cdr. Guy William Price, RNAS.
  In recognition of the gallantry and determination displayed by him in leading offensive patrols, which have constantly engaged and driven away enemy aircraft.
  On the 2nd January 1918 he observed seven Albatross scouts, and crossing the lines in the clouds, he attacked one, which fell vertically, bursting into flames, and crashed to the ground.
  He has on several other occasions driven enemy aircraft down out of control.
- Flt. Lieut. (now Flt. Cdr.) Alan Murray Waistell, RNAS.
  For the determination and pluck shown by him in carrying out a bombing raid on Chanak on the night of the 17th October 1917. In spite of the fact that there was no moon and that the weather conditions were so adverse that other pilots were unable to reach the objective, he succeeded in reaching Chanak and dropping his bombs. On the return journey he hit the side of a mountain, being unable to see it on account of the darkness, the machine catching fire on crashing. Although severely injured about the face and knee, he was able to climb out of the machine, and eventually reached the aerodrome, having ridden ten miles over extremely rough country with a badly lacerated knee.
- Flt. Lieut. (Act. Flt. Cdr) Norman Miers Macgregor, RNAS.
  In recognition of his skill and courage in aerial combats. On the 12th December 1917, whilst leading his flight on an offensive sweep, he encountered a body of six Albatross scouts at 14,000 feet. In the general fight which ensued he attacked a scout which was engaging one of our machines and drove it down out of control, and it was seen to crash.

Act. Flt. Cdr. Macgregor has destroyed several enemy machines and has led his flight with great dash and judgement.
- Flt. Lieut. Rudolph Dawson Delamere, RNAS.
  In recognition of the gallantry and devotion to duty shown by him in carrying out reconnaissance, bombing and photographic flights during the military operations in the Lindi (East Africa) area.
- Flt. Lieut. Samuel Marcus Kinkead, RNAS.
  In recognition of the conspicuous gallantry and skill displayed by him in the face of the enemy in aerial combats, notably on the following occasions:—
  On the 24th October 1917, he brought down an enemy machine, and immediately afterwards encountered and drove off a group of seven hostile aeroplanes. On the 4th December 1917, he brought down an enemy two seater machine completely out of control. By his skill and determination in attacking enemy machines he has always shown a fine example to other pilots.
- Flt. Lieut. John Foster Chisholm, RNAS
  In recognition of his services on the 6th December 1917 when he carried out a photographic reconnaissance in the vicinity of Zeebrugge, and for the great skill and determination with which he has carried out his duties at all times.
- Lieut. Evelyn Cecil Walter Fitzherbert, RNVR.
  In recognition of the valuable services performed by him as observer in the RNAS during the military operations in East Africa. His reports on the country, enemy positions etc. and his photographs have been of the greatest assistance to the operations.
- Flt. Sub. Lieut. Ronald McNeill Keirstead, RNAS.
  In recognition of conspicuous gallantry in aerial combats.
  On the 24th September 1917, he engaged single handed four enemy aeroplanes, of which two were destroyed by him. On the 21st October 1917, during an engagement between a British and a German formation, he attacked one of the enemy scouts and shot its port wings away from the rest of the machine. He then dived on to some enemy scouts which were attacking another of our machines and brought one of them down in a spinning nose dive.
- Flt. Sub. Lieut. William Lancelot Jordan, RNAS
  In recognition of the courage and initiative displayed by him in aerial combats.
  On the 13th July 1917, in company with another pilot, he attacked an enemy two seater machine. After bursts of fire from both of our

machines, the enemy observer was seen to collapse in the cockpit and the enemy aircraft was last seen disappearing among some houses. On the 6th December 1917, whilst patrolling at 15,000 feet, he saw a two seater enemy aircraft at 10,500 feet, and dived on him, firing about thirty rounds. After falling over to the left, enemy aircraft went down vertically. He has also been instrumental in bringing down other enemy machines.

- Flt. Sub. Lieut. Harold Day, RNAS
In recognition of the skill and determination shown by him in aerial combats, in the course of which he has done much to stop enemy artillery machines from working.
On the 6th January 1918, he observed a new type enemy aeroplane. He immediately dived to attack, and after a short combat the enemy machine went down very steeply, and was seen to crash.
On several other occasions he has brought down enemy machines out of control.

The KING has been graciously pleased to approve of the award of the Distinguished Service Cross to the undermentioned Officers of the British Mercantile Marine in recognition of zeal and devotion to duty shown in carrying on the trade of the country during the war:—
LG 22.2.1918 p 2305.

- Capt. Francis William Chambers
- Capt. Thomas Henry Clatworthy
- Capt. Paul Egbert George
- Capt. Edwin George Humby
- Capt. Charles Mathews
- Capt. George Shearer
- Capt. Henry Thomas Shilling
- Capt. David Mason Taggart
- Capt. William Tinmouth
- Ch. Offr. John Herbert Carter
- Ch. Offr. Charles Nugent St. Clair
- Ch. Engr. David Alexander Young
- 2nd Offr. Otto Henry Bohner

The KING has been graciously pleased to approve of the award of the Distinguished Service Cross to Officers for services in Destroyer and Torpedo Boat Flotillas during the period ending 31st December 1917:—
LG 8.3.1918 pp 2977/8

- Lieut. Frederic Thornton Peters, DSO, RN
- Lieut. Edward Chicheley Thornton, RN
- Lieut. Walter Fitzgerald Smithwick, RN
- Lieut. Frederick Edward Raw, RN
- Lieut. John Myers, RN
- Lieut. William Alexander Herlihy, RN

- Lieut. Cyril Eustace Douglas-Pennant, RN
- Lieut. Ronald James Usher, RN
- Lieut. Henry John Haynes, RN
- Lieut. Alexander Grant, RN
- Lieut. Ralph Clement Smith, RN
- Lieut. (Act Lieut. Cdr) Arthur Cocks, RNR
- Act. Lieut. Robert Don Oliver, RN
- Payr (Act. Staff Payr) Herbert Percy Hunter, RN
- Lieut. Charles Leonard Dettmar, RNR
- Lieut. John Ibbotson Harrison, RNR
- Surgn. Prob. Wilfrid Parsons Warner, RNVR
- Ch. Art. Engr. Patrick Nolan Flannigan, RN
- Ch. Art. Engr. Frederick Duckworth, RN
- Gnr. (T) Peter John Skuse, RN
- Gnr. (T) Charles James Pounds, RN
- Gnr. William Robert Lockyer, RN
- Sig. Bosn. Albert Samuel Hart, RN
- Art. Engr. Albert Henry Benfield, RN

The KING has been graciously pleased to approve of the award of the Distinguished Service Cross for services in action with enemy submarines:—
LG 8.3.1918 p 2981

- Lieut. George Gordon Dustan Salmon, RN
- Mate Claude George Rogers Hayhoe, RN

The KING has been graciously pleased to approve of the award of the Distinguished Service Cross to the undermentioned officers:—
LG 16.3.1918 pp 3393/4

Honours for Services in Action on the occasion of the raid into the Straits of Dover by enemy destroyers on the night of the 14th-15th February 1918.

- Engr. Lieut. John Abraham Kirkham, RNR
Displayed great courage and devotion to duty. His ship had been heavily shelled, was holed below water, and was settling down by the head. Engr. Lieut. Kirkham kept the pumps going as long as steam lasted, thus saving the vessel by keeping her afloat, until another vessel came to her assistance and towed her stern first into Dover harbour.
- Skpr. Henry Bennett, RNR 1013 SA (HM Trawler, "James Pond")
Displayed the utmost courage and devotion to duty. Skpr. Bennett ably assisted Ch. Skipper Berry in his efforts to save the vessel after she had been heavily shelled and set on fire. Attempts were made to put out the fire and to get up the ammunition from below, but both efforts failed, and finally the ship was abandoned. The boat was successfully launched in spite of the fact that the falls had been destroyed by the shelling. The crew got

away in her, and succeeded in effecting a landing on the French coast, where they received every attention from the French authorities.

- Skpr. Samuel Alger Head, RNR 1908 WSA, HM Drifter, "Vera Creina".
  Displayed gallantry and presence of mind in keeping his ship afloat, when badly holed by two 4 inch shells, by plugging the holes with beds and blankets.
- Skpr. John Mair, RNR 1323 WSA, HM Drifter, "W. Elliott".
  Displayed great coolness and presence of mind when his ship was sunk with the loss of seven hands and he himself was injured.
- Skpr. John Turrell, RNR 1126 WSA, HM Drifter, "Golden Rule".
  When his ship was severely damaged and ten of his crew had been killed and three badly injured, he displayed great courage and energy in giving orders to the remaining three hands although severely injured himself.

To receive a Bar to the Distinguished Service Cross.

- Lieut. Alexander Duff Thomson, DSC, RNR
  Displayed the greatest courage, coolness and devotion to duty. The vessel which he commanded was heavily shelled, and very considerable damage was done to her. The first salvo wrecked the bridge, the W.T. room, and Lieut. Thomson's cabin underneath the bridge, the Officer of the Watch being killed outright. Lieut. Thomson managed to get out of his cabin alive and made for the bridge. He maintained his coolness throughout, and after the action was over managed to get an SOS signal through to Folkestone Pier, his W.T. having been put out of action. He then examined his vessel, and found she had been holed below water, and was settling down by the head.
  At 6.30 am another vessel came to his assistance and towed his ship stern first into Dover Harbour.
- Ch. Skpr. Alfred Edward Berry, DSC, RNR, 111 SA, HM Trawler, "James Pond".
  Displayed the utmost coolness and devotion to duty, and behaved in a most courageous manner.
  His vessel was heavily shelled and set on fire. His cabin was pierced by a shell which exploded and wrecked it, wounding Ch. Skpr. Berry in the legs and setting fire to the whole of the weelhouse. He remained cool and collected throughout, immediately giving orders to all hands to lie down until the firing was over. He then made every effort to get the fires out, and although the hose had been blown to pieces, it was replaced under his directions. Both the attempt to put out the fires and to bring up the ammunition failed, and then Ch. Skpr. Berry gave orders to abandon ship.

He refused to abandon his vessel, though offered assistance by a French T.B.D. until he was convinced she was doomed. It was found that the falls of the boat had been destroyed, but the boat was successfully man handled and launched, and the crew got away in her, Chief Skipper Berry being the last to leave.

The KING has been graciously pleased to approve of the award of the Distinguished Service Cross for services in action with enemy submarines:—
LG 16.3.1918 p 3394

- Lieut. Frederick William Hawkridge, RN
- Sub. Lieut. Henry Harvey Clement Ainslie, RN

The KING has been graciously pleased to approve of the award of the Distinguished Service Cross to Officers of the Royal Naval Air Services:—
LG 16.3.1918 pp 3395/6

- Flt. Cdr. Richard Bernard Munday, RNAS
  For courage and initiative. Offensive patrols under his able and determined leadership have consistently engaged enemy aircraft and he has displayed the utmost courage in carrying out special missions alone, both by day and by night.
  On the 21st February 1918, he attacked a new type enemy two seater machine. The enemy machine dived steeply east, and Flt. Cdr. Munday followed and closed in, firing a long burst at close range, after which the enemy went down vertically out of control.
  On other occasions he has brought down enemy machines completely out of control, and has set fire to and destroyed enemy kite balloons both by day and night. On one occasion he attacked an enemy kite balloon at night and destroyed both the balloon and its shed by fire.
- Flt. Lieut. (actg. Flt. Cdr) Miles Jeffrey Game Day, RNAS (since killed).
  For great skill and bravery as a fighting pilot. On the 25th January he attacked, single handed, six enemy triplanes, one of which he shot down. On the 2nd February 1918, he attacked and destroyed an enemy two seater machine on reconnaissance at 18,000 feet.

He destroyed several enemy machines in a short space of time and in addition had numerous indecisive engagements.

- Flt. Lieut. Ernest Edward Deans, RNAS.
In recognition of great skill and bravery in flying machines of an old type in East Africa. He has carried out some very useful and long flights, and has completed his reconnaissances even when the machine has been practically uncontrollable through bumps. He has been eager and ready to go up at all times, and has shown no thought of personal danger.

- Flt. Sub. Lieut. Edward Grahame Johnston, RNAS
For the pluck and determination shown by him in engaging enemy aircraft.
On the 19th January 1918 he attacked five Albatross scouts, and engaged one, nose on, opening fire at 75 yards range. The enemy aircraft turned on its side and spun. He followed, and engaged again at 30 yards range. The enemy aircraft went down completely out of control. Later in the day in a general engagement with fourteen Albatross scouts, he followed one down to 8,000 feet, firing all the time. This is confirmed by other pilots of the patrol to have fallen completely out of control. On several other occasions he has destroyed enemy machines or brought them down completely out of control.

To receive a Bar to the Distinguished Service Cross.

- Flt. Cdr. Guy William Price, DSC, RNAS
For consistency and determination in attacking enemy aircraft, often in superior numbers.
On the 22nd January 1918, when on offensive patrol, he observed seven Albatross scouts. He dived and fired into one of the enemy aircraft, which stalled, side slipped, and eventually fell over on its back, disappearing through a thick bank of clouds, and was observed by others of our machines to fall completely out of control. On several other occasions he has destroyed enemy machines or brought them down completely out of control.

- Flt. Lieut. (act. Flt. Cdr). Wilfrid Austin Curtis, DSC, RNAS
For continuous skill and courage as a fighting pilot. On the 23rd January 1918, whilst on offensive patrol, he followed three two seater enemy machines and an enemy scout through the clouds. The enemy were then joined by five other scouts. He dived and fired into an enemy two seater from about 40 feet behind. The enemy machine fell over on its side and started to spin, and was observed by another

pilot to break up in the air while spinning down.
Since the award of the Distinguished Service Cross this officer has destroyed several enemy machines and driven down others completely out of control.

- Flt. Lieut. William Lancelot Jordan, DSC, RNAS
For skill and determination when leading offensive patrols.
On the 6th January 1918, when on offensive patrol he observed ten Albatross scouts. The enemy dived and spread out, and Flt. Lieut. Jordan, in conjunction with another pilot attacked one, into which he fired at close range, sending it down in a side slipping dive. On numerous other occasions he has attacked enemy aircraft with great dash and gallantry and has destroyed or sent them down out of control.

To receive a Second Bar to the Distinguished Service Cross.

- Flt. Cdr. Robert John Orton Compston, DSC, RNAS
For ability and determination when leading offensive patrols, in which he displays entire disregard of personal danger.
On the 1st January 1918, he observed a new type twin tailed two seater enemy machine, which he attacked, firing a good many rounds at point blank range. The enemy machine dived, but was again attacked and went down vertically with his engine full on. The wings came off, and the machine was observed to crash. Later in the day Flt. Cdr. Compston observed two formations of ten and five Albatross scouts respectively. He attacked one of the enemy machines and sent it down in a flat spin and falling over sideways completely out of control.
On numerous other occasions Flt. Cdr. Compston has destroyed or driven down enemy machines completely out of control, and has frequently had more than one successful engagement in the same day.

The KING has been graciously pleased to approve of the award of the Distinguished Service Cross to the undermentioned Officers:—

(a) For services with the Royal Naval Siege Guns in France.
LG 16.3.1918 p 3396

- Capt. Humphrey Peck, RMA
For continuous good work while in charge of a gun, and in command of its crew and camp from the 2nd February 1917, until the present

date. Previous to the formation of the RMA Heavy Siege Train, this officer was in command of a detached gun from June 1916 until February 1917. He has also been of the greatest assistance whilst acting as Adjutant of the unit from February 1917, until present date.

To receive a Bar to the Distinguished Service Cross.

- Capt. Gerald Fenwick Haszard, DSC, RMA

Has on many occasions shown an example of coolness under fire. Twice in one month when the bombardment was very heavy he went to the assistance of wounded men.

On the 15th July 1917, when a dug out was blown in by a shell, he extricated two severely wounded men under heavy shell fire and carried them to a place of safety.

On the 28th July 1917, whilst his gun position and the road adjoining were under heavy and continuous shell fire, a dump of heavy ammunition was blown up, causing a great cavity in the road. An ambulance containing a wounded officer and man fell into the shell hole. Capt. Haszard immediately went out and with the help of Gnr. Walker, RMA, who was wounded directly afterwards and died subsequently, carried the wounded officer on his back into an adjoining dug out. He then returned and brought in the wounded man.

(b) For services with the Royal Naval Transport Service in France.
LG 16.3.1918 p 3396

- Asst. Payr. (actg Payr) Reginald Charles Yorke, RNR

The KING has been graciously pleased to approve of the award of the Distinguished Service Cross to the undermentioned Officers in recognition of their services in vessels of the Auxiliary Patrol between 1st January and 31st December 1917:—
LG 6.4.1918 pp 4259/60

- Lieut. Ernest William King, RNR
- Lieut. Donald Luke Webster, RNR
- Lieut. John Percival Abernethy Richardson, RNVR
- Ch. Skpr. James Henry Brown, RNR 838 WSA
- Ch. Skpr. Thomas Albert Dawson, RNR 37 WSA
- Ch. Skpr. Edwin Charles Smith, RNR 1872 WSA
- Ch. Spr. William Wood, RNR 2551 SA
- Skpr. Henry John Alger, RNR 1898 WSA
- Skpr Ernest Edward Breach, RNR 195 WSA
- Skpr. George Crockett, RNR 2195 WSA
- Skpr. James Falconer, RNR 1170 WSA
- Skpr. Robert Sinclair Harkes, RNR 444 SA
- Skpr. John Charles Hayward, RNR 218 WSA
- Skpr. George Lewis Ormes, RNR 578 WSA
- Lieut. (act. Lieut. Cdr) Richard Cowell Coppock, RNR
- Lieut. (act. Lieut. Cdr) Keith Robin Hoare, RNVR
- Lieut. George Foote, RNR
- Lieut. Albert Arthur Crowther, RNR
- Lieut. James William Naylor, RNR
- Lieut. George Holmes, RNR
- Lieut. Helmar August Dillner, RNR
- Lieut. George Scott, RNR
- Lieut. Arthur Henry Sawdon, RNR
- Lieut. Richard Mate Jackson, RNR
- Lieut. Arthur Lakeland Sanderson, RNR
- Lieut. Arthur Hulme, RNR
- Lieut. Robert Ernest Andrews, RNR
- Lieut. Robert Jobling, RNR
- Lieut. Herbert Sutor, RNR
- Lieut. Eric Thomson Skelton, RNR
- Lieut. John Richard Charles Carter, RNR
- Lieut. Louis George Duncan Parkes, RNR
- Lieut. Richard Andrew Crafter, RNR
- Lieut. Richard Brightman Young, RNR
- Lieut. John Andrew Campbell, RNR

The KING has been graciously pleased to approve of the award of the Distinguished Service Cross to the undermentioned Officers for services in Vessels of the Royal Navy employed on Patrol and Escort duty during the period 1st January to 31st December 1917:—
LG 6.4.1918 p 4262

- Engr. Lieut. Albert William Gannaway, RN
- Lieut. Harold Auten, RNR

The KING has been graciously pleased to approve of the award of the Distinguished Service Cross to the undermentioned Officers for services in action with enemy submarines:—
LG 6.4.1918 p 4263

- Lieut. William Campbell, RNR
- Lieut. George Robert Ainslie, RNR
- Skpr. Joseph Henry Bullock, RNR 1944 SA
- Skpr. Matthew Martin Pockley, RNR 529 WSA

The KING has been graciously pleased to approve of the award of the Distinguished Service Cross to the undermentioned officer:—
LG 6.4.1918 p 4263

- Lieut. Alan Ernest Cain, RNR

The KING has been graciously pleased to approve of the award of the Distinguished Service Cross to the undermentioned Officers of the British Mercantile Marine, in recognition of zeal and devotion to duty shown in carrying on the trade of the country during the war:—
LG 6.4.1918 pp 4263/4

- Capt. John Robert Godfrey
- Capt. John Montador
- Capt. Oliver Stoker-Johnson
- Capt. Ebenezer Bow Watters
- Capt. Eowardus Vooght
- Chief Offr. Harry Pindar Barker
- Chief Offr. Richard Hodgson
- Chief Engr. Alexander Cumming
- Chief Engr. William Alexander Johnstone
- Chief Engr. William Sharp Martin
- Chief Engr. Edward Rutherford Wright

The KING has been graciously pleased to approve of the award of the Distinguished Service Cross to the undermentioned Officers in recognition of their services in minesweeping operations between the 1st April and 31st December 1917:—
LG 17.4.1918 pp 4643/4

- Lieut. Francis Howard, RN
- Lieut. Geoffrey Henry Hughes-Onslow, RN
- Lieut. Henry Heath Wood, RNR
- Lieut. Walter Leonard Cook, RNR
- Lieut William Armstrong Westgarth, RNR
- Lieut. William Highton, RNR
- Lieut. William Worrall, RNR
- Lieut. Walter James Tomkins, RNR
- Lieut. James Trenance, RNR
- Lieut. Charles Waterland Read, RNR
- Lieut. Martin Smith, RNR
- Lieut. Geoffrey Thomas Whitehouse, RNR
- Lieut. John Henry James, RNR
- Lieut. James Walker Stephen, RNR
- Lieut. John Mitchell, RNR
- Lieut. Harold Sapsworth, RNR
- Lieut. John Henry Owen, RNR
- Lieut. Edward John Dawes, RNR
- Lieut. Oswald Franklin Pennington, RNR
- Lieut. David McClymont, RNR
- Lieut. Herbert Klugh, RNVR
- Lieut. Edwin George Cole, RNVR
- Engr. Lieut. John Black, RNR
- Engr. Lieut. William Shand Archibald, RNR
- Asst. Payr. (Act. Payr.) Louis Needham, RNR
- Engr. Sub. Lieut George Keaner Brown, RNR
- Ch. Bosn. Ernest Albert Griffin, RN
- Ch. Skpr. John Ballard, RNR 7 WSA
- Ch. Skpr. Edwin Barlow, RNR 78 WSA
- Gnr. Walter George Collingwood Crouch, RN

- Act. Art. Engr. Richard Henry Thomas, RN
- Skpr. George James Richard Worledge, 745 WSA
- Skpr. Harry Roberts, RNR 488 WSA
- Skpr. William Cooke, RNR 678 WSA
- Skpr. William Bell, RNR 1447 WSA
- Skpr. William Henry Bevan, RNR 1400 WSA
- Skpr. William Brown, RNR 537 WSA
- Skpr. Robert Buchan, RNR 618 WSA

To receive a Bar to the Distinguished Service Cross.
- Lieut. Arthur Edgar Buckland, DSC, RN

The KING has been graciously pleased to approve of the award of the Distinguished Service Cross to the undermentioned Officers in recognition of their services in submarines:—
LG 17.4.1918 pp 4645/6

- Lieut. Hugh Richard Marrack, RN
- Lieut. Richard Ivor Pulleyne, RN
- Lieut. Frank Percival Busbridge, RN
- Lieut. Denis William Boyd, RN
- Lieut. Reginald John Brook-Booth, RN
- Art. Engr. George Arthur Rickaby, RN

The KING has been graciously pleased to approve of the award of the Distinguished Service Cross to Officers for services in action with enemy submarines:—
LG 17.4.1918 p 4646

- Flt. Lieut. Harry Laurence Nunn, RNAS
- Skpr. Roderick Ralph, RNR 2017 WSA

To receive a Bar to the Distinguished Service Cross.
- Lieut. Harold Owen Joyce, DSC, RN

The KING has been graciously pleased to approve of the award of the Distinguished Service Cross to the undermentioned Officers:—
LG 17.4.1918 p 4646

- Lieut (now Lieut. Cdr) John Norman Tait, RN
  In recognition of his services as Navigating Officer of one of HM Ships during an attack on the Naval Works at Ostende on the 22nd September 1917.
- Surg. (actg. Staff Surg.) Armin Gascoigne Vavasour Elder, RNVR
  In recognition of his services in connection with Naval ambulance trains and sea hospital transport throughout the war. Act. Staff Surgeon Elder was frequently under fire at the Gallipoli beaches.

The KING has been graciously pleased to approve of the award of the Distinguished Service Cross to Officers of the Royal Naval Air Service:—
LG 17.4.1918 p 4647

- Flt. Lieut. (Actg. Flt. Cdr) Cyril Burfield Ridley, RNAS
For distinguished services as a pilot and for courage in low flying expeditions during which he attacked enemy trenches with machine-gun fire from a height of 30 feet.
On the 9th March 1918, he attacked a formation of enemy scouts, selecting one which was attacking one of our machines. The enemy aircraft dived down with a quantity of smoke issuing from it, but appeared to flatten out at 2,000 feet and disappeared into the mist. He has previously destroyed several enemy machines, and has at all times led his flight with great skill and courage.
- Act. Flt. Cdr. Cyril Fraser Brewerton, RNAS
- Obs. Hector Albert Furniss, RNAS
For the skill and courage displayed by them in carrying out many long and valuable photographic reconnaissances over enemy territory, particularly over Ostende, on the 21st February 1918.
- Lieut. Bertie Arthur Millson, RNAS
For the skill and courage displayed by him in carrying out two successful bombing raids on Bruges Docks on the night of 17th-18th February 1918. This officer has taken part in many night bombing raids.
- Flt. Lieut. John De Campbourne Paynter, RNAS
For the good work performed by him during a bombing attack on Ostende Seaplane Base on the 3rd March 1918, carried out in spite of very adverse weather conditions. He has shown great zeal and courage as a fighting pilot, having destroyed several enemy machines, and been twice wounded in aerial combats.
- Flt. Lieut. Frederick George Horstman, RNAS
For good services rendered in a bombing attack on Ostende Seaplane Base on the 3rd March 1918, when many direct hits were made. The raid was carried out in spite of very adverse weather conditions. He has also shown skill and courage as a fighting pilot during many engagements with the enemy.
- Flt. Sub. Lieut. Maxwell Hutcheon Findlay, RNAS
For the courage and daring displayed by him as a pilot. On the 8th March 1918, whilst on patrol, he engaged an Albatross scout, firing effectively from very close range. The enemy aircraft went down completely out of control.

He has also destroyed or driven down out of control many other enemy machines.
- Flt. Sub. Lieut. John Melbourne Mason, RNAS
For consistently good work performed in the course of numerous bombing raids on enemy aerodromes. On the 18th February 1918, he obtained a direct hit on a shed of the Varssenaere Aerodrome. On the return journey, during a fight with enemy aircraft, his control wire was shot away, but he succeeded in safely landing his machine.
- Flt. Sub. Lieut. Thomas Arthur Warne-Browne, RNAS
- Obs. Sub. Lieut. Frederick Stratton Russell, RNAS
For the skill and determination displayed by them on the 18th March 1918, when carrying out a reconnaissance over Bruges and Blankenberghe under heavy anti-aircraft fire. Both these officers have taken part in many reconnaissances over the enemy's lines, often in face of heavy anti-aircraft fire and attacks by hostile aircraft, and have always displayed great gallantry and determination.
- Obs. Sub. Lieut. Frederick Harry Stringer, RNAS
For the zeal and ability shown by him as observer in many daylight bombing attacks over enemy territory, especially on the 26th February 1918, when a direct hit was made on Engel Dump.

To receive a Bar to the Distinguished Service Cross.
- Flt. Cdr. Cecil Hill Darley, DSC, RNAS
For zeal and determination in carrying out numerous night bombing raids on enemy aerodromes,docks etc. On the night of the 18th-19th February 1918, he carried out two attacks on the St. Denis Westrem Aerodrome.
- Flt. Lieut. Valentine Edgar Sieveking, DSC, RNAS
For skill and determination in attacking enemy aerodromes, docks, etc. with bombs.
On the night of the 17th-18th February 1918, he carried out two bombing attacks on Bruges Docks, and on the following night he again carried out two attacks, one on St. Denis Westrem Aerodrome, and one on Bruges Docks. His zeal and determination cannot be too highly praised.
- Flt. Lieut. Stanley Wallace Rosevear, DSC, RNAS
For the skill and gallantry displayed by him on the 15th March 1918, when he attacked a formation of eight enemy aircraft, destroying two of the enemy machines. This officer has destroyed numerous enemy machines and is a very skilful and dashing fighting pilot.

To receive a Second Bar to the Distinguished Service Cross.
- Act. Flt. Cdr. Richard Pearman Minifie, DSC, RNAS

For courage and daring in the face of the enemy, particularly on the 13th March 1918. On that date, when on patrol with four machines, he attacked an enemy patrol of five scouts, destroying two, whilst a third was destroyed by another officer.
Act. Flt. Cdr. Minifie has now destroyed numerous hostile machines.

The KING has been graciously pleased to approve of the award of the Distinguished Service Cross to the undermentioned Officers in recognition of distinguished services performed in difficult circumstances and during a long period in British submarines operating in the Baltic Sea:—
LG 26.4.1918 p 5057.

- Lieut. Basil Nugent Downie, RN
- Mate John Pitt White, RN

To receive a Bar to the Distinguished Service Cross.
- Lieut. Douglas Carteret Sealy, DSC, RN

The KING has been graciously pleased to approve of the award of the Distinguished Service Cross to Officers for services in action with enemy submarines:—
LG 26.4.1918 p 5058

- Lieut. Sydney Pratt, RNR
- Lieut. Robert Wilson Baty, RNR
- Flt. Lieut. John Robert Crouch, RNAS
- Eng. Lieut. Walter Clare, RNR
- Skpr. William Buchan, RNR 2226 WSA

To receive a Bar to the Distinguished Service Cross
- Skpr. George Hubert Cecil Gray, DSC RNR 1558 WSA

The KING has been graciously pleased to approve of the award of the Distinguished Service Cross to the undermentioned Officers for operations on the Belgian Coast.
LG 26.4.1918 p 5058

- Lieut. Llewellyn Vaughan Morgan, RN
- Lieut. Arthur Wardell-Yerburgh, RN
- Payr. John McLeod More, RN

The KING has been graciously pleased to approve of the award of the Distinguished Service Cross to Officers of the Royal Naval Air Service in recognition of their services at Dunkirk:—
LG 26.4.1918 p 5059

- Sqdrn. Cdr. Christopher Draper, RNAS
- Sqdrn. Cdr. Anthony Rex Arnold, RNAS
- Sqdrn. Cdr. William Laurie Welsh, RNAS
- Flt. Lieut. (Act. Flt. Cdr) Fred Everest Banbury, RNAS

The following awards of the Distinguished Service Cross have been approved.
LG 26.4.1918 p 5060

- Sqdn. Cdr. Arthur Bruce Gaskell, RNAS
In recognition of his services on the occasion of the evacuation of the Thermi aerodrome on the 9th to 15th October 1917, under continuous bombardment by the enemy.
- Flt. Lieut. (Act. Flt. Cdr) Leonard Henry Rochford, RNAS
For consistent determination, bravery and skill as a fighting pilot and flight commander. He has destroyed and driven down out of control many enemy machines.
- Flt. Lieut. James Alpheus Glen, RNAS.
For exceptional gallantry and skill as a fighting pilot and flight leader. On the 7th July 1917, he attacked two seaplanes off Ostend. In conjunction with other pilots he shot down one which crashed into the sea. The second he attacked himself, and after a short combat it also crashed into the sea, sinking immediately. He has destroyed and driven down out of control many enemy machines.
- Flt. Lieut. Arthur Treloar Whealy, RNAS
For the most consistent determination, bravery and skill with which he has carried out numerous low flying harassing attacks on the enemy's troops, transports, etc. inflicting heavy casualties and damage. By his splendid example and gallantry, a great many hostile operations were hampered and frustrated. He has further brought down many enemy machines.
- Flt. Lieut. Aubrey Beauclerk Ellwood, RNAS
For the determination and skill displayed by him as a pilot. On the 10th March 1918, he attacked three Albatross scouts. He drove two of the enemy aircraft down and then dived on the third and fired a long burst. The enemy machine pulled up, fell over on its side and fell straight down out of control until lost to sight. He has also destroyed or brought down out of control many other enemy machines.

To receive a Bar to the Distinguished Service Cross.

- Flt. Lieut. Samuel Marcus Kinkead, DSC, RNAS.
For the skill and courage displayed by him as a pilot. On the 22nd March 1918, he attacked and drove down out of control an Albatross scout which was attacking a French machine. He has brought down many other enemy machines. He is an exceptionally good pilot and a clever and plucky fighter, and has performed very fine work, both on offensive patrols and on low flying missions.
- Flt. Lieut. Euan Dickson, DSC, RNAS.
For conspicuous gallantry in attacking enemy aircraft and in carrying out bombing raids. On the 16th March 1918, he went to the assistance of a machine of his formation which was being attacked at close quarters by twelve enemy scouts. Despite the fact that all the guns on his machine were useless owing to lack of ammunition, he turned and charged the hostile formation, splitting it up and diverting their attention from the other machine, thus undoubtedly saving it. On other occasions he has brought down enemy machines and taken part in many daylight bombing raids, at all times showing utter fearlessness and great determination.
- Obs. Lieut. Cyril Chapman, DSC, RNAS
In recognition of his services on the 21st March 1918 when he carried out successful spotting for the bombardment of Ostend. On other occasions he has carried out valuable reconnaissances for the Fleet.

The KING has been graciously pleased to approve of the award of the Distinguished Service Cross to the undermentioned Officers of the British Mercantile Marine in recognition of zeal and devotion to duty shown in carrying on the trade of the country during the war:—
LG 26.4.1918 p 5061

- Capt. Frederick Hanbury Gething
- Capt. William Leask
- Capt. Henry James Smith
- Capt. Gilbert Wilton
- 2nd Offr. William Atkinson Clingly
- 3rd Engr. Laurence Cuthbert Hemy

The KING has been graciously pleased to approve of the award of the Distinguished Service Cross to Officers of the Royal Naval Air Service for zeal and devotion to duty from the period 1st July to 31st December 1917:—
LG 1.5.1918 pp 5281/2

- Flt. Cdr. Gilbert George Herbert Cooke, RN

- Flt. Cdr. William George Sitwell, RN
- Flt. Cdr. William Hayland Wilson, RNAS
- Flt. Cdr. Eustace de Courcy Hallifax, RNAS
- Flt. Cdr. William Frith Horner, RN
- Flt. Lieut. (actg. Flt. Cdr) Basil Edward Pease Gregg, RNAS
- Flt. Lieut. (actg. Flt. Cdr.) John Keith Waugh, RNAS
- Flt. Lieut. (actg. Flt. Cdr) Charles Gilmour, RNAS
- Flt. Lieut. Wilfred Underhill, RN
- Flt. Lieut. Cyril Campbell Carlisle, RNAS
- Flt. Lieut. Francis Neville Halsted, RNAS
- Flt. Lieut. Leopold Howard Wilkins, RNAS
- Flt. Lieut. Rupert Samuel Montague, RN
- Flt. Lieut. Edward Garden Hopcraft, RNAS
- Flt. Lieut. Kenneth Foster Saunders, RNAS
- Flt. Lieut. Sidney Enfield Taylor, RNAS
- Flt. Lieut. Cecil Henry Fitzherbert, RNAS
- Flt. Lieut. Dennis Knowles, RNAS
- Flt. Lieut. Frederick Stanley Mills, RNAS
- Flt. Lieut. Garrett Michael Farrell O'Brien, RNAS
- Flt. Lieut. Thomas O'Connor, RNAS
- Flt. Lieut. Arthur Roach Thomas Pipon, RNAS
- Flt. Sub. Lieut. (actg. Flt. Lieut.) Edward Errol Maitland-Heriot, RNAS
- Flt. Sub. Lieut. Norman Hargreave Woodhead, RNAS

The KING has been graciously pleased to approve of the award of the Distinguished Service Cross to the undermentioned Officers:—
LG 17.5.1918 p 5855

Honours for Services in Action with Enemy Submarines.

- Lieut. John Stockton Rogers, RNR

The KING has been graciously pleased to approve of the award of the Distinguished Service Cross to the undermentioned Officers in recognition of their services in vessels of the Auxiliary Patrol abroad between 1st January and 31st December, 1917:—
LG 17.5.1918 pp 5855/6

- Lieut. Harry Liddell Mack, RNR
- Lieut. Duncan Rodger Boyd, RNVR
- Lieut. Geoffrey Richard Purcell Gilpin, RNVR
- Skpr. William Wilson, RNR 1409 WSA
- Skpr. George Thomson, RNR 2156 WSA

The KING has been graciously pleased to approve of the award of the Distinguished Service Cross to Officers of the Royal Naval Air Service:—
LG 17.5.1918 p 5856

(i) For services in Mesopotamia:—

● Lieut. Gilbert Dirk Nelson, RNVR
For the great courage and devotion to duty displayed by him as engineer officer of his detachment. He was untiring in his work, in spite of attacks of malaria and dysentery, and the successful running of the engines was due to him.

● Flt. Sub. Lieut. John Douglas Hume, RNAS (since killed).
For continuous good patrol work, artillery spotting, feeding Kut-el-Amara, etc. sometimes making three trips a day under all weather conditions. He invariably displayed great coolness and resource in the face of the enemy, regardless of personal danger.

To receive a Bar to the Distinguished Service Cross:—

● Sub. Lieut. Wilfred Henry Dunn, DSC, RNAS
For conspicuous courage and skill in carrying out an extraordinary amount of flying, both in sea and land planes. He is invariably cheerful and ready when called on for work.

● Flt. Lieut. Vivian Gaskell Blackburn, DSC, RNAS
For services in the advance and retreat from Ctesiphon, when he performed most excellent work.

(ii) Miscellaneous

To receive a Bar to the Distinguished Service Cross:—

● Flt. Cdr. Charles Philip Oldfield Bartlett, DSC, RNAS
For conspicuous bravery and devotion to duty in carrying out bombing raids and in attacking enemy aircraft.
On the 28th March 1918, he carried out three bombing raids. Whilst returning from one of these missions he was attacked at a height of about 2,500 feet by three enemy triplanes, and five other scouts. One of these he drove down, attacking it with his front guns, whilst his observer shot down out of control a second. Observing that two of the triplanes were diving on him and converging, he side slipped his machine away with the result that the two enemy machines collided and fell to the ground together, where they burst into flames. He has carried out very many bombing raids and brought down several enemy machines, invariably showing the greatest skill and determination.

● Flt. Lieut. (Act. Flt. Cdr.) Leonard Horatio Slatter, DSC, RNAS
For distinguished service rendered during a bombing attack on Ostende Seaplane Station on the 26th March 1918, when, in spite of intense anti-aircraft fire and the glare of numerous searchlights, he descended to 400 feet over his objective to drop bombs. Flt. Cdr. Slatter is a leader of unqualified keenness and dash and possessed of exceptional courage and judgement.

The KING has been graciously pleased to approve of the award of the Distinguished Service Cross to the undermentioned Officers in recognition of their services with the Naval Armoured Car Squadron during the Russian retreat from Galicia in July and August 1917:—
LG 17.5.1918 pp 5856/7

● Lieut. William Noel Lucas-Shadwell, RNVR
When the Galician campaign of 1917 opened, he led a car many times into action on the first and subsequent days. During the first day of the retreat he took his car far beyond the Russian lines against the enemy. His car was destroyed by a shell and he was wounded for the second time, but crawled back to the Russian trenches, where he rallied two companies of Russians, until too exhausted to go on. His courage, industry and attention to detail deserve great praise.

● Lieut. Walter Leonard Crossing, RNVR
Did duty in the Russian trenches opposite Brzezany and during the retreat in cars, showing great courage and cool judgement.

● Lieut. Francis Charles Bruce Lefroy, RNVR
Acted as Transport Officer to the Force during the Galician retreat. So successful was his work that not a single ounce of stores was lost, although he had unexpectedly to evacuate two hospitals and to assist the Russians in the removal of much material. On one occasion Lieut. Lefroy was without sleep for four days and four nights.

The KING has been graciously pleased to approve of the award of the Distinguished Service Cross to the undermentioned officers for services in the Mediterranean Station.
LG 17.5.1918 pp 5857/8

● Lieut. (now Lieut. Cdr.) Patrick Harry Mackenzie, RN
● Payr. (act. Staff Payr.) George Arthur Patrick Webster, RN
● Lieut. Guy Onslow Lydekker, RN
● Lieut. Arthur Ronald Farquhar, RN
● Lieut. Robert Maurice Stopford, RN
● Lieut. Robin Edmund Jeffreys, RN
● Lieut. Harold Percy Keeley, RN
● Lieut. Walter Cyprian Battle, RNR

- Engr. Lieut. Peter Harvey, RNR
- Bos's James Manby Waller, RN
- Ch. Art. Engr. Richard John Figgins, RN
- Skpr. William Innes (b), RNR 1184 WSA

The following awards of the Distinguished
Service Cross have been approved for
miscellaneous services.
LG 17.5.1918 p 5860

- Act. Lieut. Roderick Edward Francois McQuhne Mackenzie, RN
- Gnr. (T) John Guthrie Dewar, RN
The KING has been graciously pleased to
approve of the award of the Distinguished
Service Cross to the undermentioned Officers
of the British Mercantile Marine in recognition
of zeal and devotion to duty shown in carrying
on the trade of the country during the war:—
LG 17.5.1918 p 5861

- Capt. Thomas Harrison Cooper
- Capt. John Dempster
The following award of the Distinguished
Service Cross has been approved:
LG 3.6.1918 p 6533

- Lieut. Stanley Napier Blackburn, RN

The KING has been graciously pleased to
approve of the award of the Distinguished
Service Cross to the undermentioned Officers
for services in action with enemy
submarines:—
LG 7.6.1918 p 6769

- Lieut. George Leslie Harold Dean, RNR
- Lieut. Thomas Kippins, RNR
- Lieut. William Murray (b) RNR
- Lieut. Marshall Reay, RNR
- Lieut. Philip Ogwen Hughes, RNR
- Lieut. George Brotherton Morgan, RNR
- Skpr. George William Alexander, RNR 962 WSA
- Skpr. John Henry Lawrence, RNR 188A
- Skpr. George Ernest Stubbs, RNR 837 WSA
- Skpr. Andrew Walker, RNR 850 WSA
- Skpr. Arthur Oswald Whatling, RNR 996 WSA

To receive a Bar to the Distinguished Service
Cross.
- Lieut. Charles Henry Hudson, DSC, RNR
- Sub. Lieut. Donald McMillan, DSC, RNR.

The KING has been graciously pleased to
approve of the award of the Distinguished
Service Cross to Officers in recognition of their
services in vessels of the Auxiliary Patrol in
Foreign waters betwen 1st January and 31st
December 1917:—
LG 7.6.1918 p 6770

- Lieut. James Milligan, RNR
- Lieut. Malcolm Muirhead, RNR

The KING has been graciously pleased to
approve of the award of the Distinguished
Service Cross to the undermentioned
Officers:—
LG 7.6.1918 pp 6770/1

- Lieut. Viscount Maidstone, RNVR
For services with the Royal Naval Siege Guns
on shore in Flanders from December 1915 to
August 1917. During this period he showed an
utter contempt of danger and the greatest
devotion to duty. As Plotting Officer he quickly
acquired the necessary technique, combining
with it, sound judgement and a sense of
responsibility which rendered his work
absolutely reliable. On one occasion, his gunpit
being destroyed by enemy fire, he showed
marked ability in handling ratings with courage
and decision.
- Lieut. George Davis, RNR
For skill and bravery shown by him in
recovering enemy mines.
- Lieut. Edward Hilton Young, MP, RNVR
For services with one of the most advanced
Royal Naval Siege Guns on shore in Flanders
from July 1917, to February 1918.
For many months the gun-pit and adjoining
camp were subjected to continual heavy fire
from machine-guns and guns of the largest
calibre. The conduct and example of this
officer during these arduous times was beyond
all praise, and he displayed qualities of
leadership of the highest order. His gun was
brought into action with skill and promptitude,
and it was due to his example that the splendid
morale of the ratings under him was
maintained.
- Eng. Lieut. Ernest Miller Fittock, RN.
For the coolness and promptitude shown by
him in keeping the engines of one of HM ships
working at high speed when the ship had been
holed in the engine room below the water line
in action off the Belgian coast.
- Act. Lieut. Basil Baseby, RMA
In recognition of his services with the RMA
Siege Guns in Flanders. On 18th March 1918,
an enemy shell entered the right gunpit,
dismounting the gun and causing a fire. Lieut.
Baseby had been gassed the previous evening,
and was still on the sick list, but at once
proceeded to the gunpit, and by his example
and personal efforts extinguished the fire,
which might otherwise have reached the
ammunition in the ready magazine. The battery
was under heavy shell fire at the time. He has

at all times displayed zeal, cheerfulness, and ability.

The KING has been graciously pleased to approve of the award of the Distinguished Service Cross to Officers of the Royal Naval Air Service:—
LG 7.6.1918 pp 6771/2

- Flt. Lieut. John Gamon, RNAS
  For conspicuous gallantry and devotion to duty. On the 30th March 1918, whilst returning from a bombing raid, he was attacked by three enemy triplanes, one of which he brought down and drove off the other two. He has carried out very many bombing raids on enemy lines of communication, aerodromes, and dumps. His work has always been of the greatest merit, and he has set a splendid example to those around him.
- Flt. Sub. Lieut. George Brown Sievwright McBain, RNAS
  For conspicuous bravery and devotion to duty in carrying out bombing raids on enemy troops, aerodromes, and lines of communication. On the 18th March 1918, while returning from bombing an enemy aerodrome, he was attacked by five enemy scouts. After a short combat one of the scouts was seen to nose dive, and its tail plane fell off. The four other enemy aircraft retired. He has carried out many bombing raids, at all times showing great determination, and setting a splendid example.

To receive a Bar to the Distinguished Service Cross.
- Flt. Lieut. (act. Flt. Cdr.) Leonard Henry Rochford, DSC, RNAS
  For consistent determination, bravery and skill. As a Flt. Cdr. he has shown considerable ability, and has always set a fine example when dealing with enemy aircraft. On the 21st March 1918, when on offensive patrol, he attacked one of nine Albatross scouts. Enemy aircraft was seen to go down in the mist out of control. He has destroyed or driven down out of control many other enemy machines.
- Flt. Lieut. (act. Flt. Cdr.) Charles Roger Lupton, DSC, RNAS.
  For conspicuous bravery and skill in leading bombing formations, especially on 26th March 1918, when he carried out at low altitudes four bombing raids on enemy communications. In the course of these raids he caused great damage to enemy transport, and inflicted serious casualties on large numbers of their reinforcements. He has carried out very many bombing raids, and by his courage and

resource has instilled a spirit of confidence and daring in all those who have flown with him.
- Flt. Lieut. James Alpheus Glen, DSC, RNAS
  For exceptional gallantry and skill as a Flight Leader when engaging enemy aircraft. He has destroyed or driven down out of control many enemy machines.

The KING has been graciously pleased to approve of the award of the Distinguished Service Cross to the undermentioned Officers of the British Mercantile Marine, in recognition of zeal and devotion to duty shown in carrying on the trade of the country during the War:—
LG 7.6.1918 p 6772

- Capt. John Banks Allan
- Capt. Edward John Hughes
- Capt. Charles Reginald King, (Lieut. Cdr. RNR)
- Capt. William Lobb
- Capt. William McCone
- Capt. James Edward Prettyman
- Capt. Samuel Shaw
- Capt. William Ferrie Wood

The KING has been graciously pleased to approve of the award of the Distinguished Service Cross to the undermentioned Officers for services in the action with enemy destroyers off the Belgian Coast on the 21st March 1918.
LG 21.6.1918 p 7301/2

- Lieut. David Graham Horndon Bush, RN, HMS "Botha".
  For the extremely cool and able manner in which he controlled gunfire. His orders were given with precision, and he was quick to seize the opportunity to shift to a better target. There was no hitch whatsoever in the control, and this was entirely due to his very careful organisation and training of control parties. Made preparations to be taken in tow with admirable promptitude.
- Lieut. Basil Rupert Willett, RN
  Showed the greatest courage and judgement in an attack made on five enemy destroyers after they had broken off the engagement with the "Botha" and "Morris", scoring a direct hit with a torpedo on one of these vessels.
- Art. Eng. Evan Edward Wellman, RN
  For the exceptional coolness and initiative shown by him when, early in the action, a shell damaged the auxiliary steam pipes of HMS "Botha". When escaping steam prevented the watch keepers from making their escape from the boiler room affected, Art. Eng. Wellman isolated the compartment by closing stop valves from the upper deck, the ship being

under heavy fire at the time. By this action he saved the lives of the men and assisted them to escape.

The KING has been graciously pleased to approve of the award of the Distinguished Service Cross to the undermentioned Officers for services in action with enemy submarines:—
LG 21.6.1918 p 7303

- Lieut. Cyril Ernest Remington Alford, RN
- Lieut. James Fullarton, RNR
- Lieut. William Watkin Thomas, RNR
- Lieut. James Stevenson Allan, RNR
- Lieut. Joseph Stephen Bell, RNVR
- Skpr. Ernest Robert Browne, RNR 2007 WSA

The KING has been graciously pleased to give orders for the award of the Distinguished Service Cross for services in the Patrol Cruisers under the command of Vice Admiral Sir Reginald G. O. Tupper, K.C.B., C.V.O., and Vice Admiral Sir Montague E. Browning, K.C.B., M.V.O., during the period 1st January to 31st December 1917:—
LG 21.6.1918 p 7303

- Lieut. Joseph Arthur Wallis, RNR
- Sub. Lieut. Charles John Leonard Hayward, RNR
- Asst. Payr. Thomas Johnston Elliott, RNR

The KING has been graciously pleased to approve of the award of the Distinguished Service Cross to the undermentioned Officers:—
LG 21.6.1918 pp 7303/4

- Surg. Henry Brice Parker, M.B., RN
In recognition of the exceptionally good work done by him as Medical Officer of the Nelson Battalion, Royal Naval Division, in Gallipoli.
- Lieut. Leslie Thompson, RNR
In recognition of his services in submarines.

The KING has been graciously pleased to approve of the award of Bars to the Distinguished Service Cross to the undermentioned Officers late of the Royal Naval Air Service:—
LG 21.6.1918 p 7304

To receive a Bar to the Distinguished Service Cross.
- Lieut. (tempy. Capt.) Stearne Tighe Edwards, DSC, RAF.
For conspicuous bravery and most brilliant leadership of fighting patrols against enemy aircraft. On the 2nd May 1918, whilst leading a patrol of four scouts, he encountered a hostile formation of eight enemy scouts, and drove down one enemy machine completely out of control. Soon afterwards he engaged another formation of six enemy scouts, driving down one to its destruction whilst his patrol accounted for another. He only broke off the fight owing to lack of ammunition. He has destroyed or driven down out of control many enemy machines since he was awarded the Distinguished Service Cross, and has at all times shown the greatest gallantry and a fine offensive spirit.
- Lieut. (Hon. Capt.) Arthur Roy Brown, DSC, RAF.
For conspicuous gallantry and devotion to duty. On the 21st April 1918, while leading a patrol of 6 scouts he attacked a formation of 20 hostile scouts. He personally engaged two Fokker triplanes, which he drove off; then, seeing that one of our machines was being attacked and apparently hard pressed, he dived on the hostile scout, firing the while. This scout, a Fokker triplane, nose dived and crashed to the ground. Since the award of the Distinguished Service Cross he has destroyed several other enemy aircraft and has shown great dash and enterprise in attacking enemy troops from low altitudes despite heavy anti-aircraft fire.
- Lieut. (Hon. Capt.) Arthur Treloar Whealy, DSC, RAF.
For conspicuous gallantry and devotion to duty. He has proved himself to be a brilliant fighting pilot. Under his able and determined leadership his flight has engaged and accounted for many enemy machines, he himself being personally responsible for many of these.

To Receive a Second Bar to the Distinguished Service Cross.
- Lieut. (temp. Capt.) Thomas Frederick Le Mesurier, DSC, RAF.
For gallantry and consistent good work. He has at all times displayed the utmost gallantry in action, and by his determination and skill has set a very fine example to the pilots of his squadron. On the 23rd April 1918, in spite of bad weather conditions, he successfully dropped bombs on the Ostend Docks from a height of 800 feet amidst very intense anti-aircraft and machine-gun fire. He also made valuable observations. He has taken part in many bomb raids, and has destroyed or driven down out of control several enemy machines.

The KING has been graciously pleased to approve of the award of the Distinguished Service Cross to the undermentioned Officer of the British Mercantile Marine, in recognition of zeal and devotion to duty shown in carrying on the trade of the country during the war.
LG 21.6.1918 p 7304

● Capt. Henry Arthur Yardley

The KING has been graciously pleased to give orders for the award of the Distinguished Service Cross to the undermentioned Officers:—

In recognition of distinguished services during the operations against Zeebrugge and Ostend on the night of the 22nd-23rd April 1918:—
LG 23.7.1918 pp 8588/90

● Lieut. Francis John Lambert, RN ("Thetis")
Carried out his duties with perfect coolness and judgement under very heavy fire. Although gassed, he showed great bravery in returning from the boat to "Thetis", after she had been abandoned, to look for an officer, who, he supposed, had been left behind.

● Lieut. Victor Alexander Charles Crutchley, RN ("Brilliant")
Showed great coolness under heavy fire, and set a fine example to his men. He at once volunteered on hearing that another operation was in contemplation.

● Lieut. Alan Cory Wright, RN ("Intrepid").
Showed great coolness during the action, and by his bravery and cheerfulness throughout set a fine example to his men.

● Lieut. Cuthbert Francis Bond Bowlby, RN.
In command of a coastal motor boat. Showed great coolness under very heavy fire, stopping his boat abreast the seaplane sheds at a range of 60 to 70 yards, and continued firing, making numerous direct hits.

● Lieut. Philip Edward Vaux, RN ("Iphigenia")
Performed valuable services as navigating officer in a position of considerable danger, at times under heavy fire.

● Act. Lieut. George Devereux Belben, RN ("Thetis").
Carried out his duties with perfect coolness and judgement under very heavy fire. On abandoning "Thetis", he took charge of the overcrowded boat, which was holed and partially waterlogged, and handled her most ably, keeping her afloat until picked up by a motor launch.

● Eng. Lieut. Wilfrid Long, RN ("Brilliant")

Whilst his ship was under very heavy fire approaching the position where she was to be sunk, this officer showed great bravery, and by his devotion to duty set a fine example to his men.

● Eng. Lieut. William Richard McLaren, RN ("Sirius")
Rendered great services in "Sirius" during the operations off Ostend. After "Sirius" had been sunk, pulled thirteen miles out to sea with ten men of "Sirius", so as to avoid capture. Volunteered for the second operation as soon as he knew it was contemplated.

● Surg. William Little Clegg, MB, RN, ("Vindictive")
Was in charge of the stretcher parties on the upper deck of "Vindictive". Landed on the mole to recover casualties. Later, when he was proceeding with his party along the forward mess deck of "Vindictive", a shell entered and burst close to him, killing one of his stretcher bearers. He continued his work immediately and by his personal example kept his stretcher parties going.

● Lieut. Leonard James Lee, RNVR
Volunteered for specially dangerous work in charge of machine-guns in a motor launch. Took command when the commanding officer was killed and the vessel so damaged that she had to be sunk to avoid capture. Showed great coolness, setting a fine example to his men in spite of a severe wound.

● Lieut. James Courtenay Keith Wright, RNVR
Second in command of HM Motor Launch 282. Showed great courage and coolness in embarking the crews of "Intrepid" and "Iphigenia". It was largely due to the magnificent manner in which he and others carried out their duties that so many officers and men were rescued from the blockships in the canal at Zeebrugge. He was dangerously wounded during the operation.

● Lieut. John William Robinson, RNVR, 2nd in command of HM Motor Launch 424.
When the captain was killed and the vessel completely disabled, Lieut. Robinson took command. He got the wounded and crew away in the dinghy and destroyed the motor launch by setting fire to the engine room. Showed great coolness throughout.

● Lieut. Arthur Gerald Bagot, RNVR, 2nd in command of HM Motor Launch 283.
Showed great coolness under fire. It was largely due to the magnificent manner in which the officers and men of Motor Launch 283 carried out their duties that so many officers

and men of "Brilliant" and "Sirius" were rescued.

- Lieut. George Frederick Bowen, RNVR, 2nd in command of HM Motor Launch 110.
  When the captain was killed and the vessel completely disabled Lieut. Bowen took command, got the wounded and crew away in the dinghy and sank the motor launch by firing the Lewis gun through the bottom of each compartment. Showed great coolness throughout.

- Lieut. Malcolm Stuart Kirkwood, RNVR
  Volunteered for rescue work and showed coolness and courage throughout the operations off Ostend. After his vessel was damaged alongside Brilliant, and the engineers gassed, he went down to the engine room, which was full of fumes, and started the starboard engines, thereby saving the vessel from being either sunk or captured. Shortly afterwards he lost consciousness and was rescued with difficulty.

- Act. Lieut. Harold Vivian Rogers, RNR, Navigating Officer of "Daffodil".
  Throughout the operations was of the greatest assistance, performing any duty required of him with promptness and fearlessness in an exposed position, and at times under very heavy fire. When his commanding officer was temporarily incapacitated by wounds, took command of the ship, and did everything possible to ensure the safety of the ship and crew.

- Sub. Lieut. Credric Robert Leonard Outhwaite, RNVR.
  In command of a Coastal Motor Boat. Under considerable gunfire from shore defences, torpedoed an enemy destroyer proceeding eastward from Zeebrugge harbour.

- Mate (E.) Sidney Graville West, RN, ("Iphigenia").
  Throughout the preparations and the operation this officer worked his department in an admirable manner. After the alarm bell for blowing the charges had been rung he returned to the engine room in order to start the engines ahead, and did not finally leave until he received an order from the commanding officer to do so. He was thus of the greatest assistance in the accurate placing of the blockship.

- Lieut. Charles Robert Wharram Lamplough, RMLI.
  Was in the Marine storming party. In spite of great difficulties, showed the greatest dash and determination in leading his men. He covered the retirement with great resource.

- Lieut. George Underhill, RMLI.
  Was in the Marine storming party. Showed great coolness and courage. At a critical time he organised and led reinforcements with the greatest dash and contempt of danger. His action was of the utmost value to the success of the operation.

- Act. Sub. Lieut. (Act) Peter Booth Clarke, RNR
  In command of a Coastal Motor Boat. Showed great coolness and courage under very heavy fire, returning to "Sirius" after she had been abandoned to look for an officer and some men who, it was thought, had been left behind. He handled his boat with marked ability.

- Act. Sub. Lieut. (Act) Leslie Robert Blake, RNR
  In command of a Coastal Motor Boat. Led an attack on enemy vessels moored inside the mole at Zeebrugge with skill and coolness under heavy fire from the shore defences. His boat, though damaged, was successfully brought back into harbour.

- Act. Sub. Lieut. (Act) Alfred Victor Knight, RNR ("Sirius").
  Showed great coolness under heavy fire, and was most useful throughout the operation. He at once volunteered on hearing that another operation was in contemplation.

- Gnr. (T) Thomas William Galletly, RN ("North Star").
  Took charge of his gun with coolness and ability under a very heavy fire until it was put out of action. He showed an energetic example to the men, and successfully evacuated all the wounded before abandoning ship, she being in a sinking condition and continually hit.

- Art. Eng. William Mark Sutton, RN ("Daffodil")
  Displayed wonderful leadership and devotion to duty. At the commencement of the operations it appeared doubtful whether sufficient head of steam could be kept in the boilers to enable "Daffodil" to perform the duties required. Mr. Sutton's untiring exertions, initiative and resource enabled this difficulty to be overcome. Throughout the pushing operation he managed to maintain 160 lbs. of steam, a pressure which would have seemed impossible in view of previous experience. The engine room was holed and two compartments flooded, but these were immediately and efficiently dealt with by Mr. Sutton.

- Act. Art. Eng. William Henry Edgar, RAN. ("Iris II")
  It was due to this officer that the ship was kept going during the action under very heavy fire, and though holed several times, succeeded in returning to base under her own steam. He did invaluable work in the engine room and boiler

room throughout the operation for a period of seventeen hours without rest. He showed great bravery when ship was under very heavy fire, by coming on to the upper deck, and with the help of an engine room artificer turned on the smoke apparatus.

- Serjt-Maj. Charles John Thatcher, RMLI
Was mainly instrumental in conveying the heavy scaling ladders from the ship to the Mole and throughout the operation displayed great coolness and devotion to duty.
To receive a Bar to the Distinguished Service Cross.
- Lieut. Edward Lyon Berthon, DSC, RN ("Sirius")
This officer accompanied Lieut. Cdr. Hardy to look for an Engineer Lieut. and some men, who, it was thought, had been left behind. This was done under heavy and accurate fire from 4.1 inch and machine-guns.
- Sub. Lieut. Maurice Charles Humphrey Lloyd, DSC, RN, ("Iphigenia"). (Since died of wounds).
Showed great coolness under heavy fire, and by his bravery and devotion to duty, set a fine example to his men. On abandoning ship, after she had been sunk, Sub. Lieut. Lloyd was severely wounded. This very gallant young officer has since died of wounds.

The KING has been graciously pleased to approve of the award of the Distinguished Service Cross to the undermentioned Officer in recognition of his gallantry in the action between HM Torpedo Boat Destroyers "Mary Rose" and "Strongbow", and three German light cruisers which attacked a convoy on the 17th October 1917:—
LG 7.8.1918 p 9337

- Act. Lieut. John Richard Dudley Freeman, RN
Gallantly performed his duty in charge of a 4 inch gun in HMS Mary Rose while in action against superior forces.

The KING has been graciously pleased to approve of the award of the Distinguished Service Cross to the undermentioned Officers:—
LG 7.8.1918 p 9338

Honours for Service in Action with Enemy Submarines.
- Eng. Lieut. Edward Jones, RNR
- Act. Lieut. William Philip Lillie, RN
- Mid. David Henry Millward, RNR
- Ch. Skpr. George Herbert Treece Birch, RNR 951 WSA

The KING has been graciously pleased to approve of the award of the Distinguished Service Cross to the undermentioned Officer:—
LG 7.8.1918 p 9339

Honours for Miscellaneous Services.
- Lieut. (act. Capt.) John Herbert Hollingsworth, RM
In recognition of his services with the Royal Naval and Royal Marine Artillery siege guns in Flanders from November 1916, to May 1918. During this period he has displayed great zeal and devotion to duty, and has done very valuable work in ranging the heavy guns mounted in the sector.

The KING has been graciously pleased to approve of the award of the Distinguished Service Cross to the undermentioned Officers of the Mercantile Marine in recognition of zeal and devotion to duty shown in carrying on the trade of the country during the war:—
LG 7.8.1918 p 9339

- Capt. Andrew Brown
- Capt. Frederick Galway Cadiz
- Capt. Robert Capper (Commander RNR)
- Capt. William James Campbell
- Capt. Joseph Harry Cole
- Capt. Henry Daniel
- Capt. Angus Keith
- Capt. John Lewis
- Capt. McArthur McLean
- Capt. James McNaughton
- Capt. John Roberts
- Capt. George Francis William Sim
- Ch. Off. Stewart Darragh
- Ch. Eng. Andrew Allan
- Ch. Eng. Thomas Boleyn
- Ch. Eng. George Gemmell

The KING has been graciously pleased to approve of the award of the Distinguished Service Cross to Lieut. Reginald Dundas Merriman, RIM, for valuable services in connection with the defence of Kut el Amara.
LG 23.8.1918 p 9818

- Lieut. Reginald Dundas Merriman, RIM

The KING has been graciously pleased to approve of the award of the Distinguished Service Cross to the undermentioned Officers, in recognition of the distinguished services mentioned in the foregoing despatch. (Zeebrugge 22nd to 23rd April 1918)
LG 28.8.1918 p 10089

- Sub. Lieut. James Petrie, RNVR
This officer volunteered for rescue work in ML276. When the coxswain was killed near the Ostend piers, he jumped to the wheel and steered the launch into the harbour. When fired on by machine-guns from the piers, he manned the Lewis gun and returned the fire on both pier heads. Later, when three wounded men were discovered in the water, he personally assisted them into the launch, being exposed all the time to heavy fire.
- Lieut. Albert L. Poland, RN
In command of a coastal motor boat, and carried out a successful torpedo attack on the pier ends, afterwards laying and maintaining good smoke screens close inshore throughout the remainder of the operation under heavy fire.
- Lieut. Anthony C. Mackie, RNVR
This Officer was of great assistance in command of ML279. He pluckily carried on his smoke screen work under fire for one and a half hours after breaking the starboard shaft, retiring with the rest of the flotilla, when operations were completed under one engine.
- Lieut. Felix F. Brayfield, RNVR
This Officer volunteered for rescue work as second in command of ML128. ML128 in company with ML283 went in after "Vindictive" to look for survivors. When near the shore she came under heavy fire, the signalman was killed and Lieut. Brayfield and one of the crew wounded. Lieut. Brayfield showed great devotion to duty, remaining on the bridge and carrying on with his duties until the operation was over, though wounded in the leg.
- Lieut. Allan L. Geddes, RNVR
This Officer was in command of ML553 and leader of an inshore smoke screen unit. He led his unit with skill and judgement under fire, and it was largely due to him that the smoke screen was so extremely successful in his section.
- Lieut. Rawsthorne Proctor, RNVR
This officer was in charge of a section of motor launches screening Monitors during the bombardment of the Ostend shore batteries. He exhibited conspicuous ability and initiative under heavy fire, and materially contributed to the success of the operation.
- Lieut. Russell H. McBean, RN
In command of a coastal motor boat. He escorted "Vindictive" close up to the entrance at Ostend, covering her with smoke screen and then assisting her with guiding lights. He torpedoed the eastern and western piers, and finally engaged the machine-guns there with his own machine-guns at point blank range with apparently good effect. He most skilfully handled his vessel under a heavy fire until he was wounded.
- Sub. Lieut. George R. Shaw, RNR
Second in command of a coastal motor boat which escorted "Vindictive" with smoke screen close up to the entrance of Ostend Harbour, assisting her with guiding lights. His vessel then torpedoed the eastern and western piers, and finally engaged the machine-guns at point blank range. During this engagement the commanding officer was wounded and the chief motor mechanic killed. Having seen "Vindictive" inside the piers and the work of his vessel completed, Sub. Lieut. Shaw brought her safely back to harbour.
- Lieut. William H. Bremner, RN
Was in command of a coastal motor boat. When carrying out his smoke screening of the enemy shore batteries, he encountered close inshore an enemy torpedo boat, which switched on her searchlight and opened fire. Lieut. Bremner had no better weapons then Lewis guns, but with these he attacked and peppered the torpedo boat to such good effect as to drive her away from the harbour entrance and prevent her interfering with the blocking operation.

To receive a Bar to the Distinguished Service Cross.

- Lieut. Cuthbert F. B. Bowlby, DSC, RN.
In command of a coastal motor boat and escorted "Vindictive" close up to the entrance, then ran ahead, and finding one of the piers, fired a torpedo at it. The water being shallow and the range short, the explosion shook the boat so severely as to damage her engines and open her seams. She commenced to sink, but by his presence of mind he got the leak stopped, engines going again, and brought his boat out of the fire zone, where he was taken in tow by HMS Broke.
- Lieut. The Hon. Cecil E. R. Spencer, DSC, RN.
This officer was in command of a coastal motor boat and escorted "Vindictive" close inshore and kept touch with her until she gave the last resort signal, on which he laid and lit the flare, which greatly assisted the operation, drawing heavy fire previously directed at the "Vindictive" on to himself.

The KING has been graciously pleased to approve of the following further award of the Distinguished Service Cross in addition to those announced in the London Gazette of the 23rd July 1918:—

LG 28.8.1918 p 10090

Additional Award for Services in the Operations against Zeebrugge on the night of the 22nd-23rd April 1918:—

● Act. tempy. Co. Serjt. Maj. (Warrt. Offr. 2nd Cl.) Ernest Edward Kelly, No. Ch/10068

The KING has been graciously pleased to approve of the award of the Distinguished Service Cross to the undermentioned Officers for services in action with enemy submarines:—

LG 14.9.1918 p 10847

● Lieut. John Alan Pennington Legh, RN
● Lieut. Cyril Whichelo Bower, RN
● Lieut. Gerald Roger Cousins, RN
● Lieut. Alan Duncan Leslie Macpherson, RN
● Lieut. Arthur Mallorie Coleman, RN
● Lieut. John William Townsley, RNR
● Lieut. Louis Edgar Workman, RNR
● Actg. Lieut. Edward John Grey, RNR
● Surg. Prob. George Edward Strahan, RNVR
● Asst. Payr. Athol Dalston Davis, RNR
● Act. Sub. Lieut. (Actg) George Samuel Anakin, RNR
● Art. Eng. Charles Palmer, RN
● Skpr. Richard Brouckxon, RNR 408 WFS

The KING has been graciously pleased to approve the award of the Distinguished Service Cross to the following Officers in recognition of their services on the occasion of the sortie of the "Goeben" and "Breslau" from the Dardanelles, on the 20th January 1918:—

LG 14.9.1918 p 10849

● Acting. Lieut. David Blyth Dun, RNR (HM Monitor M28)
He was sent by his Captain in the whaler to rescue men in the water. After landing them, although M28 was visibly on fire, he returned with a volunteer crew, and remained alongside until she blew up, sinking his boat.
● Flt. Sub. Lieut. Robert Withy Peel, RNAS (now Lieut. RAF)
Carried out a determined and courageous bombing attack on the Goeben in the face of attacks from a vastly superior enemy air force.
● Obs. Sub. Lieut. Frederick Charles Smith, RNAS (now Lieut. RAF)
Acted as observer for Flt. Cdr. Sorley during a determined and successful bombing attack on

the Breslau on the 20th January 1918, and also during subsequent day and night attacks on the Goeben.
● Skpr. Harry Oliver Hunn, RNR 1145 WSA HM Drifter Anchor of Hope II.
● Skpr. Benjamin George Reynolds, RNR 2114 SA, HM Drifter Supernal.
Remained on patrol in their drifters during the action and made smoke screen in a gallant endeavour to screen HM Monitors Raglan and M28, showing great presence of mind and initiative. Both vessels were invaluable in rescuing survivors.
● Lieut. Frederick Faulkner, RN (HMS Lizard)
He showed great coolness throughout the action. He got the armament into action against the Breslau, and later against destroyers, ably and quickly and soon obtained a straddle. He personally took charge of first aid party, reviving survivors, and made excellent arrangements for the custody of prisoners.
● Lieut. Arthur Jelfs Cubison, RN (HMS Tigress)
He showed marked ability as gunnery officer of the ship; straddled quickly and hit an enemy destroyer.
● Flt. Cdr. Ralph Squire Sorley, RNAS (now Tempy. Capt. RAF)
For the determined and successful bombing attacks on the Breslau and Goeben on the 20th January 1918, and subsequent days, both by day and by night.
● Surg. James Maurice Harrison, RN (HM Monitor M28)
A wounded man having fallen into the water, Surg. Harrison went in after him and kept him afloat until picked up. It was due to his untiring efforts that eight severely wounded cases arrived in good condition at the hospital ship twenty two hours later.
● Flt. Lieut. Harry Vernon Worrall, RNAS (Now Hony. Capt. RAF)
Made a successful attack on the Goeben obtaining a direct hit, although this was his first night flight.

The KING has been graciously pleased to approve of the award of the Distinguished Service Cross to the undermentioned Officers:—

LG 14.9.1918 p 10850

● Tempy. Capt. John Edward Reynolds, RM
For services with the Royal Marine Artillery Unit in German South West Africa during 1914.
● Flt. Sub. Lieut. Thomas Hinshelwood, RNAS (now Capt. RAF)
For general good work and successful long reconnaissances under fire when serving with

the Expeditionary Force in German South West Africa in 1914. Exhibited courage and resource when compelled to make a forced landing, whilst endeavouring to re-establish touch with the right advance on Olavifontein.

The KING has been graciously pleased to approve of the award of the Distinguished Service Cross to the undermentioned Officers of the Mercantile Marine in recognition of zeal and devotion to duty shown in carrying on the trade of the country during the war:—
LG 14.9.1918 p 10850

- Capt. Charles Philip Dickens
- Capt. Joseph Marcus Pearson
- Capt. William Robertson

The KING has been graciously pleased to approve of the award of the Distinguished Service Cross to the undermentioned Officers:—
LG 20.9.1918 p 11175

Honours for Services in the Auxiliary Patrol, Minesweeping and Coastal Motor Boats, between the 1st January and 30th June 1918.
- Lieut. the Hon Cecil Edward Robert Spencer, RN
- Lieut. William Rudolph Slayter, RN
- Lieut. Richard Francis John Onslow, RN
- Lieut. Charles Ronald Cameron, RNR
- Lieut. George Stuart Thomson, RNR
- Lieut. John Hugh Merifield, RNR
- Lieut. William John Holland Hall, RNR
- Lieut. John Whitefield, RNR
- Lieut. Albert Robert Williamson, RNR
- Lieut. Duncan Alexander MacKinnon Watt, RNR
- Lieut. Grant Rougvie, RNR
- Lieut. Hugh Owen, RNR
- Lieut. William Victor John Clarke, RNR
- Lieut. Louis Whitehead, RNR
- Lieut. William Wilson, RNR
- Lieut. Theodore John Butler Beard, RNR
- Lieut. George Andrew Drummond, RNR
- Lieut. Reginald Hubert Foley, RNVR
- Lieut. Samuel Rayer, RNVR
- Ch. Skpr. Horace Walter Bristow, RNR, 86 WSA
- Ch. Skpr. William Henry Maunder, RNR 498 WSA
- Ch. Skpr. Thomas May, RNR 141 WSA
- Ch. Skpr. Peter Yorston, RNR 1 WSA
- Skpr. James Johnston Donaldson, RNR 814 SA
- Skpr. George Innes, RNR 1380 WSA
- Skpr. Jim Ritchie McBeath, RNR 1772 WSA
- Skpr. George Henry Rogers, RNR 221 SA
- Skpr. (now Ch. Skpr) James Henry Smith (a) RNR 43 WSA

- Skpr (now Ch. Skpr) William John Thomas, RNR 534 WSA

The KING has been graciously pleased to approve of the award of the Distinguished Service Cross to the undermentioned Officers:—
LG 20.9.1918 p 11177

Honours for Services in Monitors and Destroyers of the Dover Patrol between the 1st January and 30th June 1918.
- Lieut. Richard Hungerford Caldwell, RN
- Lieut. Kenneth Clarke Kirkpatrick, RN

The KING has been graciously pleased to approve of the award of the Distinguished Service Cross to the undermentioned Officer:—
LG 20.9.1918 p 11178

Honours for Services in Destroyers of the Harwich Force between the 1st January and the 30th June 1918.
- Lieut. Alban Edward Trevor Tate, RN

The KING has been graciously pleased to approve of the award of the Distinguished Service Cross to the undermentioned Officer:—
LG 20.9.1918 p 11178

Honours for Services in Minesweeping Operations between the 1st January and 30th June 1918.
- Lieut. Gerald Henry Lee Jones, RNR

The KING has been graciously pleased to approve of the award of the Distinguished Service Cross to the undermentioned Officer:—
LG 20.9.1918 p 11178

Honours for Services in Local Defence Flotillas, between the 1st January and 30th June 1918.
- Lieut. William Ahern, RN

The KING has been graciously pleased to approve of the award of the Distinguished Service Cross to the undermentioned Officers:—
LG 20.9.1918 p 11178

Honours for Services in Vessels employed on Escort, Convoy and Patrol Duties between the 1st January and 30th June 1918.
- Lieut. Ernest Beeley, RN
- Lieut. Archibald Talbot Yardley, RNR
- Lieut. Norman John Gibson, RNR

The KING has been graciously pleased to approve of the award of the Distinguished Service Cross to the undermentioned Officer:
LG 20.9.1918 p 11179

Honours for Services on the Mediterranean Station between the 1st January and 30th June 1918.
- Ch. Gnr. Daniel Patrick Joseph Enright, RN

The KING has been graciously pleased to approve of the award of the Distinguished Service Cross to the undermentioned Officers:—
LG 20.9.1918 p 11179

Honours for Services on the Mediterranean Station (Egyptian Division) for the period ending the 31st December 1917.
- Lieut. Bertie Etherington Smith, RNR
- Lieut. William Brydon Chilton, RNR
- Gnr. Will Messenger, RN

The KING has been graciously pleased to approve of the award of the Distinguished Service Cross to the undermentioned Officer:—
LG 20.9.1918 p 11180

Honours for Services in Submarines between the 1st January and 30th June 1918.
- Lieut. Alfred Mark Lee, RNR

The KING has been graciously pleased to approve of the award of the following Distinguished Service Cross to the undermentioned Officer for services in action with enemy submarines.
LG 20.9.1918 p 11180

- Lieut. Herbert French Rainey, RNR

The KING has been graciously pleased to approve of the award of the Distinguished Service Cross to the undermentioned Officer:—
LG 20.9.1918 p 11180

- Eng. Sub. Lieut. Thomas Daniells, RNR

The KING has been graciously pleased to approve of the award of the Distinguished Service Cross to the undermentioned Officers:—
LG 5.10.1918 p 11779

Honours for Services in the Destroyer Action in the Adriatic on the night of the 22nd-23rd April 1918.
- Act. Lieut. George Hugh Boddie, RN
  For extreme efficiency in extinguishing fires and reorganising ship after the action. He rendered great assistance in bringing the ship safely into harbour when the commanding officer was wounded.
- Surg. Prob. Charles C. Elliott, RNVR
  He carried out his duties in attending wounded under heavy fire and difficult conditions. Although he was suffering from a painful sprained wrist, his skilful work undoubtedly saved several lives. His conduct was an example and encouragement to all on board.
- Ch. Art. Eng. Edward Charles Phillips, RN
  He entered the burning shell room accompanied by two men and rescued two wounded stokers, and afterwards by strenuous exertions succeeded in getting the fire under control and finally extinguished it.
- Gnr. George Marden, RN
  For coolness and ability in action, especially for keeping the after 4 in. gun in action when the ship was hit aft, and for taking prompt steps to get the aerial in working order.

The KING has been graciously pleased to approve of the award of the Distinguished Service Cross to the undermentioned Officers:—
LG 5.10.1918 p 11780

Honours for Services in Action with Enemy Submarines.
- Lieut. Hugh Sydney Egerton, RN
- Lieut. Leslie Lonsdale Cooper, RN
- Lieut. Claude Asquith, RNR (Prisoner of War interned in a neutral country)
- Skpr. William Addy, RNR 111 WSE
- Skpr. George Cook RNR 131 WFS
- Skpr. Sidney Hewitt, RNR 93 WSE
- Skpr. Boreas Hume, RNR 141 WFS
- Skpr. George Moston, RNR 57 WSE
- Skpr. William Joseph Parish, RNR 97 WSE
- Skpr. Robert John Syrett, RNR 50 WSE

The KING has been graciously pleased to approve of the award of the Distinguished Service Cross to the undermentioned Officers:—
LG 5.10.1918 p 11781

Honours for Services in the Auxiliary Patrol and Minesweeping between the 1st January and 30th June 1918.
- Lieut. Arnold Ernest McNab, RNR
- Lieut. Frank Ellis, RNR

The KING has been graciously pleased to approve of the award of the Distinguished Service Cross to the undermentioned Officers:—
LG 5.10.1918 p 11781

Honours for services in Minesweeping Operations between the 1st January and 30th June 1918.
- Lieut. Henry James Chapman RNR
- Eng. Lieut. Edward Walker Elliott, RNR
- Art. Eng. John Stobart, RN
- Skpr. James Gale, RNR 2774 SA
- Skpr. George Ladley, RNR 55 SA
- Skpr. Lewis Albert McCombie, RNR 299 WSA

The KING has been graciously pleased to approve of the award of the Distinguished Service Cross to the undermentioned Officer:—
LG 5.10.1918 p 11781

Honours for Services in Vessels employed on Escort, Convoy and Patrol Duties between the 1st January and 30th June 1918.
- Art. Eng. Frank Henry Knowles, RN

The KING has been graciously pleased to approve of the award of the Distinguished Service Cross to the undermentioned Officer:—
LG 5.10.1918 p 11782

Honours for Services in Local Defence Flotillas between the 1st January and 30th June 1918.
- Lieut. Frank James Couldrey, RNR

The KING has been graciously pleased to approve of the award of the Distinguished Service Cross to the undermentioned Officer:—
LG 5.10.1918. p 11782

- Capt. George T. Thompson, Trinity House Vessel "Argus".
  In recognition of the valuable work performed by him whilst employed in connection with the maintenance of the Dover Patrol.

The KING has been graciously pleased to approve of the following further award in addition to those announced in the London Gazette of the 15th September 1916:—
LG 5.10.1918 p 11782

Additonal Award for Services in the Battle of Jutland on the 31st May 1916.
- Surg. Prob. Alexander Joe, RNVR
  Medical Officer of HMS Nestor. He behaved with the greatest coolness under fire, tending the wounded single handed both in Nestor and later on board a German destroyer. His conduct was highly praiseworthy throughout.

The KING has been graciously pleased to approve of the award of the Distinguished Service Cross to the undermentioned Officers of the Mercantile Marine in recognition of zeal and devotion to duty shown in carrying on the trade of the country during the war:—
LG 5.10.1918. p 11783
- Capt. Robert Liddle Allinson
- Capt. David Peregrine

The KING has been graciously pleased to approve of the award of the following decoration to the undermentioned Officer:—
LG 29.10.1918 p 12695

Honours for Services in Submarines.
- Lieut. Ronald William Blacklock, RN

The KING has been graciously pleased to approve of the award of the Distinguished Service Cross to the undermentioned Officers:—
LG 29.10.1918 p 12696

Honours for Services in Action with Enemy Submarines.
- Lieut. George Chisholm Reed, RNR
- Lieut. William John Davies, RNR

The KING has been graciously pleased to approve of the award of the following Decoration to the undermentioned Officer:—
LG 29.10.1918 p 12696

To receive a Bar to the Distinguished Service Cross.
- Surg. Alfred Robinson MacMullin, DSC, RN
  For services with the 63rd (Royal Naval) Division in France. He worked unceasingly day and night for three days to succour the wounded. Times without number, when the enemy shelling and machine-gun fire was at its worst, he walked about in the most exposed places attending to the wounded, being utterly indifferent to his own safety. The result was that the lives of many men were saved, who might otherwise have been blown to pieces where they lay. Throughout the whole of the operations his unflinching bravery won the admiration of all who saw him.

The KING has been graciously pleased to
approve of the award of the Distinguished
Service Cross to the undermentioned Officers
of the Mercantile Marine in recognition of zeal
and devotion to duty shown in carrying on the
trade of the country during the War:—
LG 29.10.1918 p 12696

- Capt. Edward Fishwick
- Capt. William Nisbet Oliver

The KING has been graciously pleased to
approve of the award of the Distinguished
Service Cross to Officers for services in action
with enemy submarines:—
LG 29.11.1918 p 14089

- Lieut. Walter Thomas Arthur Bird, RN
- Lieut. Horace Leslie Vicary, RNR
- Lieut. Arthur James Baxter, RNR
- Lieut. Ernest Edwin Woodcock, RNR
- Lieut. Arnold Eric Peek, RNR
- Lieut. John Claude Verney Morgan, RNR

The KING has been graciously pleased to
approve of the award of the Distinguished
Service Cross to the undermentioned Officers
of Coastal Motor Boats in recognition of their
gallantry during a reconnaissance of the West
Frisian coast on the 11th August 1918:—
LG 29.11.1918 p 14090

Honours for Operations off Terschelling on the
11th August 1918.
- Lieut. Edward Rowsell Lewis, RN
Displayed great gallantry as Second in
Command of the Senior Officers boat. In the
middle of the fight he partially stripped down
and reassembled a gun in an endeavour to
bring it into action again. Lieut. Lewis, although
hit in the arms and thighs by five or six bullets,
continued his duty throughout the action with
absolute cheerfulness and without remark or
complaint.
His boat being riddled with bullets and a hole
blown in her hull by the explosion of a bomb,
was destroyed by a demolition charge. The
crew were picked up three hours later by a
Dutch torpedo boat in a very exhausted
condition.
Lieut. Lewis, in spite of his wounds and three
hours immersion in the water, showed
indomitable courage, and by his cheerfulness
kept up the spirits of his men who were nearly
exhausted.
- Lieut. Guy Leslie Cockburn, RN
For the gallantry shown by him in command of
a Coastal Motor Boat under very trying
conditions. His boat caught fire and of the

crew, two were badly wounded. Having
brought his boat to within half a mile of the
shore, Lieut. Cockburn first placed the two
wounded men in the water and then blew her
up. He managed to get the wounded, who
were unconscious, a little way towards the
shore, when Dutch seamen swam out and
brought them in.
- Lieut. Robert William Bateman, RNR
For the exceptional gallantry and courage
shown by him.
In the middle of the fight, Lieut. Bateman, who
was serving in the Senior Officers boat,
stripped down and reassembled a gun in an
endeavour to bring it into action. He
undoubtedly saved the boat by spotting bombs
as they left enemy aircraft. One bomb
exploded close to the boat and blew a hole in
her hull, and would have destroyed her if
Lieut. Bateman had not warned his
commanding officer in time for course and
speed to be altered.

The KING has been graciously pleased to
approve of the following award in addition to
those announced in the London Gazette of the
23rd July 1918:—
LG 29.11.1918 p 14091

Additional Award for Services in the Operations
against Zeebrugge and Ostend on the night of
the 22nd-23rd April 1918:—
- Act. Lieut. (now Lieut.) Leopold Joseph
Hegarty, RNR ("Daffodil")
Throughout the operations was of the greatest
assistance, performing any duty required of
him with promptness and fearlessness in an
exposed position, and at times under very
heavy fire.

The KING has been graciously pleased to
approve of the award of the Distinguished
Service Cross to the undermentioned Officer of
the Mercantile Marine in recognition of zeal
and devotion to duty shown in carrying on the
trade of the country during the war:—
LG 29.11.1918 p 14091

- Capt. Thomas McMullan

The KING has been graciously pleased to
approve of the award of the Distinguished
Service Cross to the undermentioned
Officers:—
LG 11.12.1918 p 14643

Honours for Services in Grand Fleet Destroyers
between the 1st January and 30th June 1918:—

- Lieut. Charles Ernest Hotham, RN
- Lieut. Reginald Warren Hore, RN
- Gnr. (T) John Slater, RN
- Gnr. (T) Henry Jackson Epworth, RN

The KING has been graciously pleased to approve of the award of the Distinguished Service Cross to the undermentioned Officer:—
LG 11.12.1918 p 14644

Honours for Services in other Destroyers between the 1st January and 30th June 1918.
- Eng. Lieut. George Owen Hollins, RN

The KING has been graciously pleased to approve of the award of the Distinguished Service Cross to the undermentioned Officer:—
LG 11.12.1918 p 14645

Honours for Services in the Auxiliary Patrol and Minesweeping between the 1st January and 30th June 1918.
- Lieut. James Budgen, RNR

The KING has been graciously pleased to approve of the award of the Distinguished Service Cross to the undermentioned Officers:—
LG 11.12.1918 pp 14645/6

AEGEAN
- Lieut. Gerald Charles Muirhead-Gould, RN
- Lieut. Walter Murray Blair, RNVR
- Ch. Gnr. George Harris, RN

The KING has been graciously pleased to approve of the award of the Distinguished Service Cross to the undermentioned Officer:—
LG 11.12.1918 p 14646

ADRIATIC
- Act. Eng. Lieut. Frank Austin Truckle, RN

The KING has been graciously pleased to approve of the award of the Distinguished Service Cross to the undermentioned Officer:—
LG 11.12.1918 p 14647

MINE LAYING OPERATIONS OFF THE GALLIPOLI COAST
- Lieut. Noel Charles Akers, RNVR

The KING has been graciously pleased to approve of the award of the Distinguished Service Cross to the undermentioned Officers in recognition of their services during these operations:—
LG 12.12.1918 pp 14683/4

HONOURS FOR SERVICES IN WHITE SEA OPERATIONS 1918
Modyugski Island, at the sea end of the channels leading to Archangel, was captured on 1st August 1918, after the batteries had been silenced by the Allied warships, and the town of Archangel was occupied on the 2nd August, the Bolshevik Forces being quickly and efficiently overcome and driven out of the vicinity.
Following these operations, a River Expeditionary Force was organised with local craft, armed and manned by Allied crews, and this expedition succeeded in co-operation with the military forces, in clearing the River Dwina and the River Vaga of hostile craft up to the time when Allied ships had to be withdrawn to avoid the ice, several of the principal enemy vessels being destroyed.
- Payr. Lieut. (now Payr. Lieut. Cdr.) John Geoffrey Elgar, RN, HMS "Attentive".
  Controlled the fire of 4 inch guns which assisted to silence the battery on Modyugski Island on the 1st August 1918. He also rendered most valuable services in connection with supplies during both the Archangel operations and those on the West Coast of the White Sea in July 1918.
- Act. Lieut. Royer Mylius Dick, RN
  In command of the River Gunboat "Razlyff" during the Dwina operations, he saved a number of boats and a barge from falling into the enemy's hands, the ship being repeatedly fired on. In the Tchamova operations he handled his ship with conspicuous success.
- Lieut. (actg. Lieut. Cdr) Eugene Emmanuel Frost Smith, RNR HMS "Nairana".
  For great zeal and devotion to duty. It was due to his fine navigation through narrow waters and in dense fog that the advance squadron was able to arrive off the mouth of the Dwina at the appointed time, thereby greatly facilitating the capture of Archangel.
- Lieut. Henry James Francis Cavendish, RN
  He was senior officer of the Gunboat Squadron during the Dwina operations until the arrival of HMS M25.
  His gallant conduct and capable handling of his command saved an awkward situation, and inflicted considerable known damage on the enemy.
- Act. Lieut. Edward Henry Richardson, A.M., RNR
  He showed courage and enterprise of a high order as commanding officer of the Gunboat "Advokat", during the Dwina operations.

- Gnr. William Henry Kewish, RN
  Commanded the Gunboat "Gorodok" during the Dwina operations until he was wounded, fighting her with much courage and ability.
- Bosn. Herbert Gutherless, RN
  He took charge of and organised the Paddle Minesweeping Squadron, which cleared the River Dwina of mines from Pless to Poutchouga under most difficult conditions and with the most meagre resources. He displayed very fine qualities of leadership during the landing at Tchamova.

The KING has been graciously pleased to approve of the award of the Distinguished Service Cross to the undermentioned Officers for services in action with enemy submarines:—
LG 17.1.1919 p 883

- Lieut. Bernard Talbot Chick, RNVR
- Lieut. George Hargreaves Greenwood, RNVR

To receive a Bar to the Distinguished Service Cross.
- Lieut. (act. Lieut. Cdr) Charles Herbert Lightoller, DSC, RD, RNR Lieut.
- William Brydon Chilton, DSC, RNR

The KING has been graciously pleased to approve of the following further award in addition to those announced in the London Gazette of the 15th September 1916:—
LG 17.1.1919 p 884

Additional award for Services in the Battle of Jutland on the 31st May 1916:—
- Sub. Lieut. (now Act. Lieut) Reginald Dudley Rowe, RN, Navigating Officer, HMS "Nestor". During the action was stationed on the bridge, whence he controlled the gunfire of "Nestor" with such success and cool bravery that two of the enemy's destroyers were quickly sunk and the remainder of their flotilla put to flight. This control was carried out under the heaviest fire, not only from the opposing destroyers, but from the enemy's secondary armament.

The KING has been graciously pleased to approve of the award of the Distinguished Service Cross to the undermentioned Officers:—
LG 17.1.1919 p 884

- Lieut. (now Lieut. Cdr.) William Scott Chalmers, RN
  In recognition of his services with the Horse Boats on the Belgian Canals and the Naval

Siege Guns on shore in Flanders between December 1914, and April, 1915.
He at all times displayed the seamanlike qualities of quickness and resource and personal courage of a very high order. His good example of cheerful and fearless work under the most trying circumstances contributed in a great degree to the excellent behaviour of the men.
- Capt. Henry Vincent Fuller, RM, attd. RMLC.
  On the night of the 6th-7th August 1918, during an enemy air raid, in which several huts of the RMLC were demolished or severely damaged, his conduct was an example to all. He assisted in getting the men away from the wrecked huts, bandaging the wounded, rendering every assistance possible, and showed an utter disregard for his personal safety.
- Lieut. Robert Hunter McNair, RNR
  For excellent services in command of a gun barge in the advanced posts on the North Dwina River from the 11th to 20th October, 1918. On the latter date the barge was sunk by concealed enemy fire. During this period he was in constant action with superior forces of enemy flotilla, thus affording relief to the land forces ashore, and covering their retirement from a difficult position.

The KING has been graciously pleased to approve of the award of the Distinguished Service Cross to the undermentioned Officers of the Mercantile Marine in recognition of zeal and devotion to duty shown in carrying on the trade of the country during the war.
LG 17.1.1919 p 884

- Capt. Samuel Driver
- Capt. James Matthew Eaton
- Capt. Thomas Gunn
- Capt. Arnold Sadler Hawker
- Capt. Robert Hughes
- Capt. Charles Richard Raby
- Capt. David McQueen Reid
- Capt. Frederick Owen Seaborne
- Capt. Harold James Symonds
- Ch. Engr. Claud Charles Lapsley, O.B.E.
- Ch. Engr. James Love Murray

The KING has been graciously pleased to approve of the award of the Distinguished Service Cross to the undermentioned Officers for services in action with enemy submarines:—
LG 15.2.1919 p 2358

- Lieut. Robert Vincent Mack, RN
- Lieut. Albert Edward Holland, RNR

- Act. Payr. Lieut. Ernest Gordon Driscoll, RNR
- Ch. Art. Eng. Frederick John Baker, RN

The KING has been graciously pleased to approve of the award of the Distinguished Service Cross to the undermentioned Officers in recognition of their services in minesweeping operations off the Belgian Coast, including the minefields off the ports of Ostend and Zeebrugge, between the 18th October and 8th November 1918:—
LG 15.2.1919 p 2358

- Lieut. Warwick Lindsay Scott, RNVR
  Was in command of a section of minesweepers employed bottom sweeping off Ostend. While sweep was being hove in, a mine came off foul of sweep, Lieut. Scott went aft and cut the circuit wire on outside of mine, making the mine safe. Mine was then salved.
- Lieut. Reginald Joynson, RNVR
  Displayed courage and good judgement in the work of opening up Zeebrugge, sweeping for and sinking mines in the harbour.
- Eng. Lieut. Charles Frederick Holt, RNR
  When his ship struck a mine off Ostend on the 19th October 1918, this Officer showed great courage in going into the foremost stokehold, the stokehold being full of steam and rapidly filling with water, and the ship likely to hit another mine at any moment. He also resuced a badly injured man.

The KING has been graciously pleased to approve of the award of the Distinguished Service Cross to the undermentioned Officer:—
LG 15.2.1919 p 2359

Honours for Services in Monitors off the Belgian Coast between the 1st July and 11th November 1918.
- Lieut. John Hermann Brougham, RN

The KING has been graciously pleased to approve of the award of the Distinguished Service Cross to the undermentioned Officers:—
LG 15.2.1919 p 2359

- Surg. Lieut. Walter Grimshaw Bigger, RN
  For services with the Royal Marine Artillery Siege Gun Detachment in Flanders.
  On the 29th May 1918, while he was attending to the wounded in Carnac gun position a second shell burst in embrasure. Surgeon Lieutenant Bigger continued his work with noteworthy calmness and devotion to duty. The coolness under fire displayed by this officer on other occasions has gained for him

the confidence of the officers and men under his medical charge.
- 2nd Lieut. Daniel Harding, RMA
  For services with the Royal Marine Artillery Siege Gun Detachment in Flanders.
  On the 28th March 1918, at Carnac battery near Oost Dunkirk, after extricating himself from the debris caused by an enemy shell bursting in his gun position, displayed marked coolness in attending to the wounded and assisting to extinguish a fire. Has since shown zeal and devotion to duty on all occasions.

The KING has been graciously pleased to approve of the award of the Distinguished Service Cross to the undermentioned Officers of the Mercantile Marine in recognition of zeal and devotion to duty shown in carrying on the trade of the country during the war:—
LG 15.2.1919 p 2361

- Capt. George Arthur Hope Flynn
- Capt. George McMillan
- Capt. William Charles Morgan

The KING has been graciously pleased to approve of the award of the Distinguished Service Cross to the undermentioned Officers:—
LG 20.2.1919 p 2557

Honours for services in Minelaying Submarines between the 1st July and 11th November 1918.
- Lieut. Gerald Aylmer Garnons-Williams, RN
- Lieut. Charles Stanley Sim, RNR

The KING has been graciously pleased to approve of the award of the Distinguished Service Cross to the undermentioned Officer:—
LG 20.2.1919 p 2558

Honours for Services in Submarines between the 1st July and 11th November 1918.
- Lieut. John Stewart Gilchrist Reid, RNR

The KING has been graciously pleased to approve of the following decoration to the undermentioned Officer:—
LG 20.2.1919 p 2558

Honours for Services in Destroyers of the Harwich Force between the 1st July and 11th November 1918.
- Lieut. Randolph Stewart Gresham Nicholson, RN

The KING has been graciously pleased to approve of the award of the Distinguished Service Cross to the undermentioned Officers in recognition of their services during Naval operations carried out in conjunction with Military operations in Palestine from October to December 1917:—
LG 20.2.1919 pp 2559/60

- Lieut. (now Lieut. Cdr) Melvill Willis Ward, RN, HM Monitor Raglan.
- Flt. Lieut. (act. Flt. Cdr.) Edward James Pointer Burling, RNAS (now Capt. RAF)
  Carried out very successful spotting work in connection with the bombardment of Deir Sineid. During this work he was attacked by a very fast hostile aeroplane, and it was only due to the extremely clever handling of his aeroplane that the machine was not destroyed.
- Lieut. George Brand, RNR, HM Trawler Gwenllian.
  Commanded the Drifter Flotilla which laid and maintained indicator nets off the beaches on which stores were landed. Owing to the strength of the current off the coast, the nets frequently dragged out of position, necessitating their being weighed and relaid. That this defence was kept in so satisfactory a state was due to the unremitting care and attention paid by Lieut. Brand and the hard work done by the drifter crews.
- Lieut. Harold Francis Addenbrooke-Kent, RNR, HMS Blossom.
  In recognition of his services in going into a burning ammunition dump to assist in extinguishing a fire, on the 16th October 1917.
- Skpr. Andrew Buchan, RNR 1323 S.A., HM Trawler Gwenllian.
- Skpr. James Abraham King, RNR 1528 SA, HM Drifter Twenty-eight.
  Ably assisted Lieut. Brand in laying and maintaining indicator nets off the beaches.

To receive a Bar to the Distinguished Service Cross.
- Flt. Lieut. Henry Vernon Worrall, DSC, RNAS, (now Capt. RAF)
  Carried out very successful spotting work for Requin off the Wadi Hesi.

The KING has been graciously pleased to approve of the award of the Distinguished Service Cross to the undermentioned Officer for services in action with enemy submarines:—
LG 17.3.1919 p 3591

- Lieut. Percy Shadforth Atkins, RNR

The KING has been graciously pleased to approve of the award of the Distinguished Service Cross to the undermentioned Officers:—
LG 17.3.1919 p 3591

Honours for services in Destroyers of the Grand Fleet Flotillas between the 1st July and 11th November 1918.
- Surg. Sub. Lieut. Arthur Arnold Osman, RNVR
- Gnr. (T) John George Beaumont, RN
- Lieut. Lachlan Donald MacKintosh, RN
- Lieut. Pelham Alexander Maitland, RN
- Lieut. Ivo Wyndham Laton Frewen, RN

The KING has been graciously pleased to approve of the award of the Distinguished Service Cross to the undermentioned Officers:
LG 17.3.1919 p 3592

- Lieut. Raymond Benson Stewart, RN, HMS Mounsey.
  For gallantry when HMS Otranto was wrecked on the 6th October 1918.
- Capt. Richard Burton, RMLI
  In recognition of his services as Adjt. of the Allied Naval Brigade in North Russia between the 14th August and 28th November 1918 when he carried out very difficult work in a most successful manner.
- Lieut. Daniel Fedotoff White, RNVR
  On the 18th August 1918, at Seltzo, with a few marines landed and captured an enemy battery. When acting in command of one of HM river gunboats at Borocovsko, on the 20th August 1918, in an action with enemy gunboats kept his gunboat under fire while repairing his guns in order to cover the retreat of our troopships, showing a fine example of coolness and devotion to duty. He has throughout the operations in Northern Russia done exceptionally good work as Intelligence Officer.
- Sub. Lieut. Wilfrid Edmund Warner, RN, HMS Mounsey.
  For gallantry when HMS Otranto was wrecked on the 6th October 1918.
- Skpr. John Stanley Higgs, RNR 88 SA
  In recognition of his services in the White Sea since 1916, where he has been continuously employed on Patrol work and Minesweeping.

The KING has been graciously pleased to approve of the award of the Distinguished Service Cross to the undermentioned Officers of the Mercantile Marine in recognition of zeal and devotion to duty shown in carrying on the trade of the country during the war:—

LG 17.3.1919 p 3593

- Ch. Engr. Ernest Richard Crafter
- 2nd Offr. James McDonald Dunbar

The KING has been graciously pleased to approve of the award of the Distinguished Service Cross to the undermentioned Officers for services in action with enemy submarines:—
LG 24.3.1919 p 3860

- Lieut. James Simpson, RNR
- Lieut. Francis Edward Temple-West, RNVR
- Sub. Lieut. William Edmund Liley, RNR

To receive a Bar to the Distinguished Service Cross.
- Lieut. Walter Thomas Arthur Bird, DSC, RN
- Lieut. Arnold Eric Peek, DSC, RNR

The KING has been graciously pleased to approve of the award of the Distinguished Service Cross to the undermentioned Officers:
LG 24.3.1919 p 3860

Honours for Services in Minelaying Operations between the 1st July and 11th November 1918.
- Lieut. Arthur Hugh Lloyd Terry, RN
- Lieut. Edwin Charles Carter, RNR
- Lieut. Bernard Hwfa Harrison, RNR

To receive a Bar to the Distinguished Service Cross.
- Lieut. Francis William Crowther, DSC, RN

The KING has been graciously pleased to approve of the award of the Distinguished Service Cross to the undermentioned Officers:—
LG 24.3.1919 p 3861

Honours for Services in Minesweeping Operations between the 1st July and 31st December 1918.
- Lieut. (now actg. Lieut. Cdr.) Archibald Gordon Cranmer, RNR
- Lieut. John Duncan Campbell, RN
- Lieut. Geoffrey Alan Brooke Hawkins, RN
- Lieut. George Ernest Blackmore, RN
- Lieut. William Edward Ross, RNR
- Lieut. Arthur Richard Haviland, RNR
- Lieut. Charles Wood, RNR
- Lieut. Ernest Matson Fall, RNR
- Lieut. Ernest Steere, RNR
- Lieut. Harry Terry, RNR
- Lieut. Charles Harold Daniel, RNR
- Lieut. George Syms, RNR
- Lieut. George Alexander Moir, RNR
- Lieut. Arthur Thomson, RNR

- Lieut. Bertie Warwick, RNR
- Lieut. James Ernest Eaglesham, RNR
- Lieut. Edward Briton Smallman, RNR
- Lieut. Edward Broad, RNR
- Lieut. William Henry Evans, RNR
- Ch. Skpr. John Henry Reynolds, RNR 10 SA
- Skpr. Charles Brewster, RNR 768 WSA
- Skpr. Andrew Buchan, RNR 614 WSA
- Skpr. Philip Pascoe Glanville, RNR 499 WSA
- Skpr. George William Tharrett, RNR 403 WSA
- Skpr. William Henry Quirk, RNR 151 SA

To receive a Bar to the Distinguished Service Cross.
- Lieut. (actg. Lieut. Cdr.) John H. Pitts, DSC, RNR

The KING has been graciously pleased to approve of the award of the Distinguished Service Cross to the undermentioned Officers:—
LG 24.3.1919 p 3862

Honours for Services in Coastal Motor Boats between the 1st July and 11th November 1918.
- Lieut. Frank Allan Winson Ramsay, RN
- Lieut. Richard Popkiss Chapman, RNR

The KING has been graciously pleased to approve of the award of the Distinguished Service Cross to the undermentioned Officer of the Mercantile Marine in recognition of zeal and devotion to duty shown in carrying on the trade of the country during the war:—
LG 24.3.1919 p 3863

- Capt. Clifford Lower

The KING has been graciously pleased to approve of the award of the Distinguished Service Cross to the undermentioned Officers in recognition of their services during Naval operations carried out in conjunction with Military operations in Palestine from September to November 1918:—
LG 11.4.1919 pp 4731/2

- Lieut. Norman Boyd Fleming Peploe, RN, HMS Druid.
  In recognition of the valuable assistance rendered to the Army during the operations.
- Lieut. Arthur Harvey Wells, RNVR, HM Motor Launch 248
  For excellent service in connection with the landing of stores on the coast during the advance, doing much to expedite and assist this important work upon which so much depended.

- Skpr. Joseph Harold Lowery, RNR 659 WSA, HM Armed Trawler Barnard Boyle.
Displayed zeal and performed valuable services when employed clearing the minefield off Haifa. The mines were laid shallow, while it was essential to clear a channel and anchorage with the utmost rapidity in order to land provisions for the Army.

The KING has been graciously pleased to approve of the award of the Distinguished Service Cross to the undermentioned Officers:—

Honours for Services in the Auxiliary Patrol between the 1st July and 11th November 1918.

(a) Services in Drifters, Trawlers and Yachts.
LG 11.4.1919 p 4733

- Lieut. (now act. Lieut. Cdr) Alexander Robinson, RNR
- Lieut. Ernest McKeown, RNR
- Lieut. Frederick Gale Cudbertson, RNR
- Lieut. Alexander MacLean, RNR
- Lieut. Joseph Richard Hodgson, RNR
- Lieut. Sydney Arnold Martyn, RNR
- Lieut. Grahame Gordon Alexander Deucher, RNR
- Ch. Skpr. William James Allan, RNR 1014, WSA
- Ch. Skpr. William Forman, RNR 369 WSA
- Ch. Skpr. Alfred Royal, RNR 311 WSA
- Skpr. Francis Pearsons, RNR 914 WSA
- Skpr. Frederick William Slade, RNR 1251, SA
- Skpr. James Smith, RNR 1316 WSA

(b) Services in Motor Launches.

- Lieut. (now act. Lieut. Cdr) Hugh Richard Preston, RNVR
- Lieut. Alfred Archie White, RNVR
- Lieut. Frank Afton MacCallum, RNVR
- Lieut. George Livingstone Cassady, RNVR

The KING has been graciously pleased to approve of the award of the Distinguished Service Cross to the undermentioned Officer:—
LG 11.4.1919 p 4734

Honours for Services in Sloops employed on Convoy, Escort and Patrol Duties between the 1st July and 11th November 1918.
- Actg. Lieut. Alec Dudfield, RNR

The KING has been graciously pleased to approve of the award of the Distinguished Service Cross to the undermentioned Officers:—
LG 11.4.1919 p 4734

Honours for Services in Destroyers employed on Convoy, Escort and Patrol duties between the 1st July and 11th November 1918.
- Lieut. (now act. Lieut. Cdr.) Kingsley Gordon Howe, RNR
- Lieut. George Hector Creswell, RN
- Lieut. Charles Lindsay Evan-Thomas, RN
- Lieut. Raymond George Francis Herault de Caen, RN
- Lieut. Alexander Putnam Cumming, RN
- Lieut. Leslie Mann, RNR
- Lieut. Richard George Clayton, RNR
- Ch. Art. Eng. John Chadwick, RN
- Art. Eng. James Charles Purnell, RN

The KING has been graciously pleased to approve of the award of the Distinguished Service Cross to the undermentioned Officers:—
LG 11.4.1919 p 4735

Honours for services in Local Defence Flotillas between the 1st July and 11th November 1918.
- Lieut. Alexander Maitland Donovan, RN
- Lieut. William Clarke, RNR
- Act. Sub. Lieut. William Smith Buckley, RNR

The KING has been graciously pleased to approve of the award of the Distinguished Service Cross to the undermentioned officers of the Mercantile Marine in recognition of zeal and devotion to duty shown in carrying on the trade of the country during the war:—
LG 11.4.1919 p 4736

- Capt. William John Gorley
- Capt. Arthur Hilditch
- Capt. Walter Jefferson
- Capt. Walter John Price
- Capt. Evan Thomas

The KING has been graciously pleased to approve of the award of the Distinguished Service Cross to the undermentioned Officer for services in action with enemy submarines:—
LG 22.4.1919 p 5111

- Act. Lieut. Ivor Gregor MacGregor, RNR

The KING has been graciously pleased to approve of the Distinguished Service Cross to the undermentioned Officer:—
LG 22.4.1919 p 5111

ADRIATIC
- Lieut. Sidney William Brooks, RN

The KING has been graciously pleased to approve of the award of the Distinguished Service Cross to the undermentioned Officer:—
LG 22.4.1919 p 5111

EGYPT
- Lieut. David Lambert, RNR

The KING has been graciously pleased to approve of the award of the Distinguished Service Cross to the undermentioned Officers:—
LG 22.4.1919 p 5113

- Lieut. (now Lieut. Cdr) Geoffrey Arthur Gordon Haggard, RN
  In recognition of his gallantry in HM Australian Submarine AE2 during the passage of the Dardanelles on the 25th April 1915.
- Surg. Lieut. Neville Hardcastle Smith, RN
  In recognition of the bravery and devotion to duty displayed by him in carrying out his professional duties during the battles in the Ussuri district between the 14th and 28th August 1918.
- Capt. Vincent Christopher Brown, RMA
  In recognition of his gallantry on the 10th and 12th May when in command of a detachment of Royal Marines in action in the vicinity of Pechenga.
- Capt. John Arthur Bath, RMLI
  Personally directed and controlled the firing of two of HMS Suffolk's twelve pounder guns against superior enemy forces in the battles on the Ussuri front between the 14th and 28th August 1918. Showed coolness and resource under fire.
- Gnr. John Hawke Moffatt, RN
  Displayed great coolness and precision in directing the fire of two of HMS Suffolk's twelve pounder guns during the battles on the Ussuri front between the 14th and 28th August 1918. Mr. Moffatt set a high example of bravery under fire, and when his observation post was attacked, continued to direct the fire until the enemy was close upon him, and by so doing prevented the enemy's armoured train advancing at a critical period.

To receive a Bar to the Distinguished Service Cross.
- Lieut. Lancelot Vivian Donne, DSC, RN
  First Lieutenance of HM Submarine E42 during the successful attack by that vessel on the German Battle Cruiser Moltke on the 25th April 1918. The successful attack and the subsequent skilful manoeuvering of E42 was largely due to his attention to detail and to his courage under trying conditions.

The KING has been graciously pleased to approve of the award of the Distinguished Service Cross to the undermentioned Officers for services in action with enemy submarines:—
LG 24.5.1919 p 6447

- Lieut. William Samuel Croucher, RNR

To receive a Bar to the Distinguished Service Cross.
- Lieut. John Dyson Chapple, DSC, RN

The KING has been graciously pleased to approve of the award of the Distinguished Service Cross to the undermentioned Officers:—
LG 24.5.1919 p 6447

Honours for Services in the Auxiliary Patrol between the 1st July and 11th November 1918.

(a) Services in Yachts, Trawlers, and Drifters.
- Lieut. William Dunlin, RNR
- Ch. Skpr. George Rowson, RNR 1724, WSA
- Ch. Skpr. George Wood, RNR 1350 SA

(b) Services in Motor Launches.
- Lieut. Gregory Robinson, RNVR

The KING has been graciously pleased to approve of the award of the Distinguished Service Cross to the undermentioned Officer:
LG 24.5.1919 p 6447

Honours for Services in Minesweeping Operations between the 1st July and 31st December 1918.
- Lieut. John Dagleish Hindmarsh, RNR

The KING has been graciously pleased to approve of the award of the Distinguished Service Cross to the undermentioned Officer:—
LG 24.5.1919 p 6448

- Flt. Lieut. Cecil Gordon Bronson, RNAS (now Capt. RAF)
  For carrying out a determined bombing attack on the Goeben on the 24th-25th January 1918, flying low down under heavy anti-aircraft fire.

The KING has been graciously pleased to approve of the following award in addition to those announced in the London Gazette of the 23rd July 1918:—
LG 24.5.1919 p 6448

Additional awards for Services in the Operations against Zeebrugge and Ostend on the night of the 22nd-23rd April 1918.

To receive a Bar to the Distinguished Service Cross.

- Capt. (now Maj.) John Maurice Palmer, DSC, RMLI.
  Captain Palmer landed on the Mole at Zeebrugge as 2nd in Command of C (Plymouth Company), and was on the Mole when the order to retire was given. By his great gallantry and total disregard of his own safety he was of the greatest assistance during the retirement in helping men to return to the ship. He refused to leave the Mole while any of his men were left there, and was taken prisoner in consequence.

The KING has been graciously pleased to approve of the award of the Distinguished Service Cross to the undermentioned Officers of the Mercantile Marine in recognition of zeal and devotion to duty shown in carrying on the trade of the country during the war:—
LG 24.5.1919 p 6449

- Capt. James Blaikie
- Capt. Thomas Harcus.

The KING has been graciously pleased to approve of the award of the Distinguished Service Cross to the undermentioned Officer:—
LG 27.5.1919 p 6504

- Paymaster Sub. Lieutenant (Acting Paymaster Lieutenant) Herbert George Arthur Woolley, RN
  For distinguished services on the Gallipoli peninsula and afterwards as Senior Secretary's Clerk to the Vice Admiral, Dover Patrol.

The KING has been graciously pleased to approve of the award of the Distinguished Service Cross to the undermentioned Officers:—
LG 11.6.1919 p 7511

- Lieut. John Domvile Auchmuty Musters, RN
  For distinguished services in destroyers and submarines throughout the war.
- Lieut. Marcel Harcourt Attwood Kelsey, RN
  For distinguished services whilst in command of a destroyer.
- Lieut. John Eric Wodehouse Oland, RCN
  For distinguished services in destroyers during the War.
- Sub. Lieut. William Basil Hallwood, RN
  For gallant and distinguished services throughout the War. He has been three times wounded in action.
- Surgeon Sub. Lieut. Annesley George Lennon Brown, RNVR

For the gallantry and devotion to duty displayed by him on the occasion of the torpedoing of HMS "Paxton" by an enemy submarine on the 20th May 1917.

The KING has been graciously pleased to approve of the award of the Distinguished Service Cross to the undermentioned Officers:—
LG 21.6.1919 p 7907

- Lieut. Basil Kerr, RNVR
  For distinguished services in command of a Squadron of Naval Armoured Motor cars during the Second Battle of Ypres in April 1915.
- Skipper Alfred Hazel Phelps, RNR 611 DA
  For distinguished services in salving and making safe mines washed ashore on the East Coast.
- Lieut. (now Lieut. Cdr) Geoffrey Eric Ridgeway, RN
  For distinguished services as Officer of the Watch of HMS "Birmingham" on the occasion of the sinking of the German Submarine U15 in the North Sea on the 9th August 1914.
- Lieut. Richard Frederick Hall, RN
  For distinguished services as Gunnery Lieutenant of HMS "Yarmouth".

The KING has been graciously pleased to approve of the award of the Distinguished Service Cross to the undermentioned Officer of the Mercantile Marine, in recognition of zeal and devotion to duty shown in carrying on the trade of the country during the war:—
LG 21.6.1919 p 7908

- Capt. John Irvine.

The KING has been graciously pleased to approve of the award of the Distinguished Service Cross in recognition of the services of the undermentioned Officers during the War:—
LG 27.6.1919 p 8068

- Lieut. William Pennell Stocker, RN
  For distinguished services in HMS "Galatea", 1st Light Cruiser Squadron, and in HMS "Cardiff", 6th Light Cruiser Squadron.
- Gnr. Walter John Driscoll, RN
  For distinguished services in HMS "Caledon" 1st Light Cruiser Squadron.
- Skpr. William Innes, RNR 1053 WSA
  For distinguished services during minesweeping operations.

The KING has been graciously pleased to approve of the award of the Distinguished Service Cross to the undermentioned Officers:—
LG 30.6.1919 p 8202

- Lieut. John Chevas Cumming, RNR
  For distinguished services in command of HM Trawler "Chikara", employed on minesweeping duties.
- Lieut. Edward Ford Duncanson, RNVR
  For distinguished services in command of HM Motor Launch ML13. He has been responsible for the destruction of many enemy mines, when searching mined areas at low water.
- Art. Eng. John William Jenkins, RN
  For distinguished services in HM ships "Shark" and "Fearless".

The KING has been graciously pleased to approve of the award of the Distinguished Service Cross to the undermentioned Officers:—
LG 10.7.1919 p 8737

- Lieut. (now Lieut. Cdr.) George Arthur Scott, RN
  For distinguished services in HMS "Severn".
- Lieut. Clarence Edward Stanhope Palmer, RNVR
  For distinguished services in HM Submarine E15, which was lost off Kephez Point, at the Dardanelles, on the 15th April 1915.
- Ch. Gnr. Herbert Daniel Jehan, RN
  For distinguished services in HMS "Iron Duke".
- Warrt. Shipwt. Ernest Charles Miller, MBE, RN
  For distinguished services in connection with dangerous and important salvage work.

The KING has been graciously pleased to approve of the award of the Distinguished Service Cross to the undermentioned Officers:—
LG 12.7.1919 p 8943

- Payr. Lieut. (now actg. Payr. Lieut. Cdr.) Harold Gordon Badger, RN
  For distinguished services as Observer in one of the seaplanes employed on spotting duties during the attack on the German Cruiser "Konigsberg" on the 6th and 11th July 1915.
- Gnr. Alfred John Mallett, RN
  For distinguished services during the Dwina River operations.

The KING has been graciously pleased to approve of the award of the Distinguished Service Cross to the undermentioned Officers:—
LG 17.7.1919 pp 9110/1

- Lieut. Gerald Harman Warner, RN
  For distinguished services in HMS "Dublin".
- Lieut. Felix Edward Chevallier, RN
  For distinguished services during the War. He has displayed excellent qualities of leadership in action on more than one occasion.
- Lieut. Douglas Roy Verey, RNVR (now Capt. RAF)
  For distinguished services with No. 14 Kite Balloon Section in Mesopotamia from August 1916 to February 1917.
- Flt. Sub. Lieut. Maurice Lyon, RNAS (now Capt. RAF)
  For distinguished services with No. 14 Kite Balloon Section in Mesopotamia from August 1916 to February 1917.
- Ch. Sig. Bosn. Joseph Harry Robins, RN
  For distinguished services during the War.

The KING has been graciously pleased to approve of the award of the Distinguished Service Cross to the undermentioned Officer:—
LG 31.7.1919 p 9833

- Lieut. Graham Scott Hewett, RNVR
  For distinguished services during the War.

The KING has been graciously pleased to approve of the award of the Distinguished Service Cross to the undermentioned Officer:—
LG 31.7.1919 p 9834

Honours for services in Action with an Enemy Submarine.
- Lieut. Edgar William Buchanan, RN

The KING has been graciously pleased to approve of the award of the Distinguished Service Cross to the undermentioned Officer:—
LG 11.8.1919 p 10199

- Lieut. Hugh Wilson, RNVR
  For distinguished services during the war.

The KING has been graciously pleased to approve of the award of the Distinguished Service Cross to the undermentioned Officer:—
LG 22.8.1919 p 10635

- Act. Sub. Lieut. (act.) John White Hampsheir, RNR
  In recognition of his conspicuous gallantry, coolness and skill under extremely difficult conditions in action.

The KING has been graciously pleased to approve of the award of the Distinguished Service Cross to the undermentioned Officer:—
LG 16.9.1919 p 11579

● Lieut. Douglas Montagu Branson, RN
For distinguished services during the war.

The KING has been graciously pleased to approve of the award of the Distinguished Service Cross to the undermentioned Officer:—
LG 16.9.1919 p 11582

Honours for Services in Action with an Enemy Submarine.
● Lieut. Sterling Neville Cobbold, RN

The KING has been graciously pleased to approve of the award of the Distinguished Service Cross to the undermentioned Officer:—
LG 17.10.1919 p 12779

● Lieut. Basil Gold Watney, RNVR
For distinguished services in connection with operations on the Danube.

The KING has been graciously pleased to approve of the award of the Distinguished Service Cross to the undermentioned Officers:—
LG 17.10.1919 p 12780

Honours for Services in Russia, 1919.
● Lieut. Ion Whitefoord Grove White, RN, Comdg. HMS Cricket.
Has fought and handled his ship with conspicuous gallantry and success, constantly under heavy fire.
● Lieut. Edward Templeton Grayston, RNR, Comdg. HMS Cicala.
Fought and handled his ship with conspicuous gallantry and success, constantly under heavy fire.
● Sub. Lieut. Archibald Hugh Mafeking Dunn, RN
As 1st Lieut of HMS Sword Dance, was engaged in minesweeping until his ship struck a mine. Carried out his duties efficiently in trying circumstances, and kept the morale of the ship's company up to a high standard.
● Ch. Gnr. David Heard Shepherd, RN, Comdg. HMS Step Dance. Handled his ship with great skill throughout all minesweeping operations.

The KING has been graciously pleased to approve of the award of the Distinguished Service Cross to the undermentioned Officers:—
LG 17.10.1919 p 12781

Honours for Services in Minesweeping Operations between the 1st July and 31st December 1918.
● Lieut. Charles Alfred Todd, RNR
● Lieut. Robert Strasenburgh Pearce, RNR
● Lieut. John Longsdon Garle, RNVR

To receive a Bar to the Distinguished Service Cross.
● Act. Lieut. George Gordon Rose, DSC, RNR

The KING has been graciously pleased to approve of the award of the Distinguished Service Cross to the undermentioned Officers:—
LG 17.10.1919 p 12781

Honours for Services in the Mine Clearance Force between the 1st January and 30th June 1919.
● Lieut. John Orgee, RN
● Lieut. Harry Stanley Endicott, RNR
● Lieut. David Jenkin Dwyndreath Davies, RNR
● Lieut. Albert James Blaker, RNR
● Lieut. Henry Hillcoat, RNR
● Lieut. Frank Leigh Wyatt, RNR
● Lieut. Herbert Frank Griffiths, RNVR
● Lieut. Alan Oakley Drake, RNVR
● Ch. Skpr. Thomas Hutchings Wills, RNR, 6820 DA
● Skpr. William Fancy, RNR 166 SA

The KING has been graciously pleased to approve of the award of the Distinguished Service Cross to the undermentioned Officers:—
LG 11.11.1919 pp 13745/6

Honours for services in Russia, 1919.
● Lieut. Ralph Petherbridge Martin, RN
For distinguished services in command of a gun detachment manned by seamen, which was of great assistance during the operations.
● Lieut. Meredith Stanton Spalding, RN
For distinguished services in command of the Naval Brigade throughout the operations of the 10th August 1919 and subsequent days.
● Lieut. Thomas Johnson Jones, RNR
For distinguished services under fire in HM Monitor 33. Lieut. Jones showed great zeal in preparing and perfecting the control and spotting instruments of the ship.
● Surg. Lieut. Walter Francis Raphael Castle, BA, RN.
For distinguished services during the action off Onega on the 1st October 1919, in attending to the wounded under heavy enemy fire.

- Sub. Lieut. Basil Theodore Brewster, RN
  For distinguished service as second in
  command of the Naval Gun battery.
- Sub. Lieut. Roland Hunter Blair, RN
  For distinguished services as second in
  command of HM Coastal Motor Boat No. 72 in
  the attack on Kronstadt Harbour on the 18th
  August 1919. The boat in which he was serving
  passed through the line of forts under a heavy
  fire and escorted HM Coastal Motor Boat No.
  86 out of action.
- Sub. Lieut. John Christian Boldero, RN
  For distinguished services as second in
  command of HM Coastal Motor Boat No. 31 in
  the attack on Kronstadt Harbour on the 18th
  August 1919, when the Bolshevik battleship
  "Andrei Pervozanni" was torpedoed by the boat
  in which he was serving under a very heavy
  fire.
- Sub. Lieut. Robert Leslie Wight, RN
  For distinguished services as second in
  command of HM Coastal Motor Boat, No. 86 in
  the attack on Kronstadt Harbour on the 18th
  August 1919. The boat in which he was serving
  passed through the line of forts under a heavy
  fire. She was then disabled when Sub. Lieut.
  Wight prepared her for towing and re-passed
  the line of forts singlehanded.
- Sub. Lieut. Edgar Robert Sindall, RNR
  For distinguished services as second in
  command of HM Coastal Motor Boat No. 7, in
  the attack on Kronstadt Harbour on the 18th
  August 1919. The boat in which he was serving
  piloted two other boats into the harbour
  through the forts under a heavy fire, and then
  patrolled the mouth of the harbour to cover
  their withdrawal.
- Act. Sub. Lieut. (Act.) Francis Walter Howard,
  RNR
  For distinguished services in command of HM
  Coastal Motor Boat No. 86 in the attack on
  Kronstadt Harbour on the 18th August 1919. He
  passed throug the line of forts under a heavy
  fire, but his engines broke down shortly after
  and he remained under fire and only able to
  move at very slow speed until escorted out by
  HM Coastal Motor Boat No. 72
- Act. Sub. Lieut. (Act) Norman Eyre Morley, RNR
  For distinguished services in HM Coastal Motor
  Boat No. 88 in the attack on Kronstadt Harbour
  on the 18th August 1919. This boat torpedoed
  the Bolshevik battleships Andrei Pervozanni
  and Petropavlovsk.
- Lieut. Clive Melbourne Sergeant, RMLI.
  For distinguished services in command of the
  Royal Marine landing party during the

operations on the Dvina River commencing on
the 10th August 1919.
- Mate Arthur Gunning Ingram, RN
  For distinguished services with the Naval Gun
  battery.
- Mid. Richard Nigel Onslow Marshall, RNR
  For distinguished services in HM Coastal Motor
  Boat No. 7 in the attack on Kronstadt Harbour
  on the 18th August 1919. This boat piloted two
  other boats into the harbour through the forts,
  under a heavy fire, and then patrolled the
  mouth of the harbour to cover their
  withdrawal.

To receive a Bar to the Distinguished Service
Cross.
- Lieut. Ernest William King, DSC, RNR
  For distinguished services in command of HM
  Paddle Minesweeper, "Walton Belle" at Onega
  on the 1st October 1919 when he handled his
  ship with great skill and courage under very
  trying circumstances.
- Lieut. Robert Hunter McNair, DSC, RNR
  For distinguished service at Onega on the 1st
  August 1919, when he landed from the tug
  Alku in charge of the covering and line parties.
  Honours for Services in the Caspian Sea, 1918,
  1919.

The KING has been graciously pleased to
approve of the award of the Distinguished
Service Cross to the undermentioned
Officers:—
LG 11.11.1919 pp 13746/7

- Lieut. George Maxwell Robertson, RNR
  For distinguished services in command of the
  Slava at the bombardment of Staro Terechnaya
  and subsequently in command of the "Sergie".
- Lieut. Arthur Brocklebank Lee, RNR
  For distinguished services in the "Venture" at
  the bombardment of Staro Terechnaya, and in
  action off Fort Alexandrovsk on the 21st May
  1919.
- Eng. Lieut. Thomas Gardner, RN
  For distinguished services in the "Emile Nobel"
  during the action off Fort Alexandrovsk on the
  21st May 1919.
- Surg. Lieut. Alan Andreas Cockayne, RN
  For distinguished services under fire as Medical
  Officer of the "Zoraster", "Venture", and "Emile
  Nobel" in action off Fort Alexandrovsk on the
  21st May 1919.
- Mate Alfred Maguire, RN
  For distinguished services in the Asia in action
  with Bolshevik destroyers on the 19th April
  1919, and off Fort Alexandrovsk on the 21st
  May 1919.

To receive a Bar to the Distinguished Service Cross.
- Lieut. Robert Mitchell Taylor, DSC, RN
For distinguished services in the Emile Nobel in action off Fort Alexandrovsk on the 21st May 1919.

The KING has been graciously pleased to approve of the award of the Distinguished Service Cross to the undermentioned Officer:—
LG 11.11.1919 p 13748

Honours for Services in the Mine Clearance Force between the 1st January and 30th June 1919.
- Skpr. William Isaac Catchpole, RNR 2824 SA

The KING has been graciously pleased to approve of the award of the Distinguished Service Cross to the undermentioned Officers:—
LG 11.11.1919 p 13748

Honours for Services in the Mine Clearance Force subsequent to the 30th June 1919.
- Lieut. Heneage Cecil Legge, RN
- Lieut. James Leo Fitzpatrick RNR
- Lieut. Robert Bonar Roberts, RNR
- Lieut. Duncan McLachlan, RNR
- Act. Lieut. Leonard Charles Orman, RN
- Mate Arthur George Graham, RN

The KING has been graciously pleased to approve of the award of the Distinguished Service Cross to the undermentioned Officers:—
LG 22.1.1920 p 948

Honours for Services in Russia, 1919.
- Lieut. Hugh Babington, RN (since died)
For distinguished services during operations on shore and in connection with mine laying.
- Lieut. George Ernest Coker, RN
For distinguished services in connection with mining operations.
- Lieut. Henry Crawford Macdonald, RN
For distinguished services on the occasion of the mining of HMS Myrtle on the 15th July 1919, when he displayed seamanship of a high order.
- Mid. Andrew William Eliot Welchman, RNR
For distinguished services in HM Coastal Motor Boat No. 36.

To receive a Bar to the Distinguished Service Cross.
- Ch. Gnr. Daniel Patrick Joseph Enright, DSC, RN

For distinguished services in action as Chief Gunner of the Flotilla and in charge of naval demolition parties.

The KING has been graciously pleased to approve of the award of the following decoration to the undermentioned Officer:—
LG 22.1.1920 p 948

Honours for Services in the Caspian Sea 1919.

To receive a Second Bar to the Distinguished Service Cross.
- Lieut. William Boydon Chilton, DSC, RNR
For distinguished services in command of seaplane carriers.

The KING has been graciously pleased to approve of the award of the Distinguished Service Cross to the undermentioned Officer:—
LG 22.1.1920 p 949

Honours for Services in Action with an Enemy Submarine.
- Act. Lieut. Walter Desmond Brown, RN

The KING has been graciously pleased to approve of the award of the decoration to the undermentioned Officer:—
LG 22.1.1920 p 946

Honours for Services in the Mine Clearance Force (Final)

To receive a Bar to the Distinguished Service Cross.
- Lieut. Robert Douglas King-Harman, DSC, RN

The KING has been graciously pleased to approve of the award of the Distinguished Service Cross to the undermentioned Officers:—
LG 8.3.1920 p 2860

Honours for Services in Siberia, 1919.
- Mate Horace Nowell Barnes, RN
For distinguished services on the River Steamer Kent operating on the Kama River.
- Gnr. Cedric William Clarke, RN
For distinguished services in command of the River Steamer Suffolk operating on the Kama River.

The KING has been graciously pleased to approve of the award of the Distinguished Service Cross to the undermentioned Officer:—
LG 8.3.1920 p 2861

Honours for Services in North Russia, 1919.
- Lieut. Oliver Champion, RNVR
For distinguished services as Naval Transport Officer, Onega.

The KING has been graciously pleased to approve of the award of the Distinguished Service Cross to the undermentioned Officers:—
LG 8.3.1920 pp 2861/2

Honours for Services in the Baltic, 1919.
- Lieut. (now Lieut. Cdr.) Edward Joseph Francis Price, RN
For distinguished services as Navigating Officer of HMS "Phaeton".
- Lieut. Lewis John Pitcairn Jones, RN
For distinguished services as Navigating Officer of HMS "Cleopatra".
- Lieut. James William Rivett-Carnac, RN
For distinguished services as First and Gunnery Lieutenant of HMS "Cleopatra".
- Lieut. the Hon. Trevor Tempest Parker, RN
For distinguished services as Gunnery Officer of HMS "Dragon".
- Lieut. Philip Miles Filleul, RN
For distinguished services in connection with intelligence work, and on the occasion of the loss of HMS "Verulam".
- Lieut. William Ogilvy Scrymgeour-Wedderburn, RN
For distinguished services as Second in Command of HM Submarine, L11.
- Lieut. William Charles Pascoe Crabb, OBE, RN
For distinguished services as Gunnery Officer of HMS "Phaeton".
- Lieut. Hugh Ernest Hollond, RN
For distinguished services as Fire Control Officer in HMS "Valorous".
- Lieut. Arthur Lovat Fraser, RNR
For distinguished services in connection with minesweeping operations.
- Lieut. Albert Travers Black, RNVR
For distinguished services in connection with minesweeping operations.
- Lieut. Trevor Louth, RNVR
For distinguished services on the occasion of the mining of HMML 156.
- Eng. Lieut. William Davidson, RNR
For distinguished services on the occasion of the mining of HMS "Banbury".
- Sub. Lieut. John Oliver Campbell, RN
For distinguished services on shore at Riga.
- Sub. Lieut. Neville Lionel John Pisani, RN
For distinguished services on shore at Riga.
- Gnr. (T) Charles Edward Coles, RN
For distinguished services in HMS "Dragon".
- Warrt. Shipwt. George Percy Byrne, RN

For distinguished services in HMS "Curacoa".
- Warrt. Teleg. Edward Clifford Dean, RN
For distinguished services in HM Ships "Curacoa", "Cleopatra", and "Delhi".

The KING has been graciously pleased to approve of the award of the Distinguished Service Cross to the undermentioned Officer:—
LG 8.3.1920 p 2864

Honours for Services in the Mine Clearance Force.
- Warrt. Eng. William Edward Henry King, RN

The KING has been graciously pleased to approve of the award of the Distinguished Service Cross to the undermentioned Warrant Officer:—
LG 23.4.1920 p 4716

- Gnr. George Thompson Jebbett, RN
For distinguished services on the occasion of the mining of HMS "Verulam" in the Baltic.

The KING has been graciously pleased to approve of the award of the Distinguished Service Cross to the undermentioned Officer:—
LG 4.5.1920 pp 5099/100

- Sub. Lieut. Osman Cyril Horton Giddy, RN
For distinguished services as second in command of HM Coastal Motor Boat 24A in the attack on Kronstadt Harbour on the 18th August 1919.

His Majesty the KING has been graciously pleased to approve of the award of the following decoration to the undermentioned Officer:—
LG 6.7.1920 p 7228

To receive a Bar to the Distinguished Service Cross.
- Lieut. Norman Boyd Fleming Peploe, DSC, RN
For distinguished services on board the Russian Ice Breaker "Donskoi Gerla" during the evacuation of the British Military Mission from Taganrog.

The KING has been graciously pleased to approve of the award of the Distinguished Service Cross to the undermentioned Officer:—
LG 7.9.1920 p 9055

- Lieut. Bernard John Littledale, RN

The KING has been graciously pleased to approve of the award of the Distinguished Service Cross to the undermentioned Officers:—
Honours for Service in Asia Minor, 1920
LG 14.1.1921 p 375

- Act. Sub. Lieut. Walter James Melrose, RN
- Mid. Norman Vincent Dickinson, RN

The KING has been graciously pleased to approve of the award of the Distinguished Service Cross to officers of His Majesty's Navy and of the Mercantile Marine in recognition of their services at Wanhsien, Yangtse River, China, on the 5th September, 1926, and connected events.
LG 6.5.1927 p 2958

- Lieut. Jack Peterson, RN, HMS Kiawo
  For special gallantry and leadership of the after boarding party from HMS Kiawo.
- Capt. Alexander Craig Thomson, Mercantile Marine, S.S. "Wanhsien".
  Held the bridge of the S.S. "Wanhsien" until the arrival of HMS "Kiawo". Later showed considerable bravery in returning without escort to recover the S.S. "Wanhsien" and "Wantung". It was largely due to his initiative, enterprise and good seamanship that the S.S. "Wanhsien" which could not raise steam was brought away lashed alongside the S.S. "Wantung".

The KING has been graciously pleased to approve of the award of the Distinguished Service Cross to the undermentioned officer in recognition of his gallant conduct on the occasion of the seizure by pirates and subsequent sinking of the S.S. "Irene" in Bias Bay on the 20th October 1927:—
LG 3.6.1929 p 3681

- Lieut. (now Lieut. Cdr.) Frederick John Crosby Halahan, RN

The KING has been graciously pleased to approve of the undermentioned awards for gallant and distinguished services rendered in connection with the emergency operations in Palestine during the period 15th April to 14th September 1936.
LG 6.11.1936 p 7122

- Lieut. Peter William Gretton, RN.

The KING has been graciously pleased to approve the following award of the Distinguished Service Cross in respect of services on the Yangtse river in December 1937:—
LG 2.12.1938 p 7606

- Mr. Joseph William Hurst, OBE, Admiralty Pilot, Yangtse River.
  On the morning of the 5th December 1937, during the bombing of British shipping at Wuhu, Mr. Hurst took control of the Tug "Ohanyung", displaying remarkable powers of command over a panic stricken native crew. By his seamanlike and fearless handling of the Tug he made possible the rescue of the ship's company of S.S. "Tuckwo" from a difficult and dangerous situation.

Index

Booker, C. D. 29
Booth, A. J. 39
Boswell, H. G. 28
Boultbee, H. T. 32
Boutillier, J. W. le 30
Bowack, E. W. 20
Bowen, G. F. 58
Bower, C. W. 61
Bowlby, C. F. B. 57, 60
Boyd, D. R. 52
Boyd, D. W. 49
Boyd, J. L. 17
Boyle, A. H. 23
Brackley, H. G. 22
Brade, F. T. 23
Bradley, J. P. 36
Brand, G. 69
Brandon, A. F. 38
Branson, D. M. 75
Bray, H. J. 15
Brayfield, F. F. 60
Breach, E. E. 48
Breadner, L. S. 24
Breese, G. F. 37
Bremner, W. H. 60
Brewer, W. H. 28
Brewerton, C. F. 50
Brewill, A. W. L. 10
Brewsher, P. 39
Brewster, B. T. 76
Brewster, C. 70
Bristow, H. W. 62
Britten, J. A. 12
Britton, T. F. 41
Broad, E. 70
Bronson, C. G. 72
Brook-Booth, R. J. 49
Brooke, J. 24
Brooke, J. C. 31
Brooke-Webb, A. C. 7
Brooks, S. W. 71
Brooksmith, E. S. 28
Brouckxon, R. 61
Brougham, J. H. 68
Broughton, V. L. D. 15
Brown, A. 59
Brown, A. G. L. 73
Brown, A. R. 38, 56
Brown, G. K. 49
Brown, G. S. 17
Brown, J. 41
Brown, J. H. 48
Brown, L. O. 28
Brown, R. 5
Brown, V. C. 72
Brown, W. 49
Brown, W. D. 77

Browne, E. R. 56
Browne, M. C. 8
Browning, T. A. 34
Bruce, J. 30
Bruce, W. (1386WSA) 15
Bruce, W. (1486WSA) 34
Bryant, F. H. 40
Buchan, A. (1323SA) 69
Buchan, A. (614WSA) 70
Buchan, R. 49
Buchan, W. 51
Buchanan, E. W. 74
Buckland, A. E. 19, 49
Buckley, W. S. 71
Budgen, J. 66
Bullock, J. H. 48
Buret, T. J. C. 41
Burgon, C. S. 39
Burling, E. J. P. 69
Burns, J. 33
Burton, J. H. 3
Burton, R. 69
Busbridge, F. P. 49
Bush, D. G. H. 55
Bush, E. W. 12
Buss, H. A. 37
Butcher, O. A. 35
Butler, C. H. 11
Butler, R. C. 32
Butler, R. W. 12
Butlin, C. M. 39
Byrne, G. P. 78

Cadbury, E. 18
Cadiz, F. G. 59
Cadman, J. 8
Cain, A. E. 48
Cain, T. E. 28
Caldwell, R. H. 62
Calvert, J. E. 30
Cameron, A. G. 32
Cameron, C. R. 62
Campbell, J. A. 48
Campbell, J. D. 70
Campbell, J. O. 78
Campbell, J. S. 20
Campbell, W. 48
Campbell, W. J. 59
Cantener, C. L. 9
Cantlie, C. 7
Capper, R. 59
Capps, W. A. 30
Cardwell, R. 24
Carew, G. 4
Carey, M. 15
Carlisle, C. C. 52
Carnduff, H. J. 12

Carpenter, G. 8
Carr, J. A. 37
Carrow, J. H. 17
Carruthers, R. J. 10
Carter, A. W. 35
Carter, E. C. 70
Carter, J. H. 45
Carter, J. R. C. 48
Cartwright, C. W. 6
Case, H. K. 16
Casey, D. A. 18
Casey, F. D. 29
Cassady, G. L. 71
Casswell, A. H. S. 6
Castle, W. F. R. 75
Catchpole, W. I. 77
Catto, A. Y. 34
Cavendish, H. J. F. 66
Cayrol, R. L. M. 9
Chadwick, A. J. 33
Chadwick, J. 71
Chafer, A. H. 30
Chalmers, W. S. 67
Chambers, C. F. M. 42
Chambers, F. W. 45
Champion, O. 78
Chaplin, B. 30
Chapman, C. 42, 52
Chapman, C. M. S. 2, 37
Chapman, H. J. 64
Chapman, R. P. 70
Chappell, L. S. 30
Chapple, J. D. 12, 72
Charlewood, C. J. 4
Chase, C. K. 21
Chater, J. D. G. 24
Cheetham, J. 5
Chevallier, F. E. 74
Chick, B. T. 67
Childers, E. 21
Chilton, W. B. 63, 67, 77
Chisholm, J. F. 44
Chittenden, A. 18
Chubb, J. W. A. 6
Churchill, J. E. 18
Cintré, A. L. M. 8
Clare, W. 51
Clarke, C. W. 77
Clarke, I. N. C. 22, 36
Clarke, M. L. 12
Clarke, P. B. 58
Clarke, W. 71
Clarke, W. V. J. 62
Clatworthy, T. H. 45
Clayton, R. G. 71
Clegg, W. L. 57
Clements, E. H. 30

Dudfield, A. 71
Dudley, A. D. 19
Duggan, W. G. 19
Dun, D. B. 61
Dunbar, J. McD. 70
Duncan, I. J. 32
Duncan, J. E. M. 15
Duncanson, E. F. 74
Dunlin, W. 72
Dunn, A. H. M. 75
Dunn, W. H. 44, 53
Dunning, E. H. 11
Durham, R. S. 30
Duthie, A. N. 15

Eaglesham, J. E. 70
Eason, V. C. G. 31
Eaton, J. M. 67
Edgar, W. H. 58
Edwards, C. C. R. 21
Edwards, K. 20
Edwards, S. T. 37, 56
Egerton, H. S. 63
Egford, G. H. 3
Elder, A. G. V. 49
Elfert, J. H. R. 21
Elgar, J. G. 66
Elliott, A. S. 37
Elliott, C. C. 63
Elliott, E. W. 64
Elliott, T. J. 56
Ellis, F. 63
Ellwood, A. B. 51
Elwell, R. G. 36
Endicott, H. S. 75
England, T. H. 17
Enright, D. P. J. 63, 77
Enstone, A. J. 33
Epworth, H. J. 66
Esteva, J. P. 9
Evan-Thomas, C. L. 71
Evans, B. 39
Evans, D. 35
Evans, G. 11
Evans, J. H. 35
Evans, W. H. 70
Evill, D. C. S. 14

Falconer, J. 48
Fall, E. M. 70
Fall, J. S. T. 24, 42, 42
Fancy, W. 75
Fane, G. W. R. 18
Farquhar, A. R. 53
Farquhar, W. 34
Farquharson, K. R. 23
Farrell, T. J. 32

Farrow, J. W. 24
Faulkner, F. 61
Faulkner, G. H. 35
Faurie, E. V. 9
Fawell, C. L. 20
Feilman, G. A. 36
Ferguson, G. 19
Ferguson, H. J. 5
Figgins, R. J. 54
Filleul, P. M. 78
Filmer, C. B. L. 24
Findlay, M. H. 50
Finlayson, A. 30
Fisher, P. S. 22
Fishwick, E. 65
Fittock, E. M. 54
Fitzgibbon, D. F. 39
Fitzherbert, C. H. 52
Fitzherbert, E. C. W. 44
Fitzpatrick, J. L. 77
Flannigan, P. N. 45
Fleming, W. St. C. 19
Flett, W. E. 23
Flynn, G. A. H. 68
Foley, R. H. 62
Follett, E. 32
Foote, G. 48
Forbes, A. (175SA) 39
Forbes, A. (66WSA) 28
Forbes, H. M. S. 12
Forman, W. 71
Forster, H. L. 43
Foster, W. 23
Fowle, F. G. 14
Fowler, A. C. 37
Fowler, F. 22
Frame, W. H. 37
Fraser, A. L. 78
Fraser, F. E. 29
Freeman, C. T. 17
Freeman, J. R. D. 59
Freer, G. F. D. 6
Frewen, I. W. L. 69
Frodsom, W. 30
Fry, H. C. C. 15
Fullarton, J. 56
Fuller, H. V. 67
Fulton, J. J. 28
Furniss, H. A. 50
Furnival, H. W. 15

Galbraith, D. M. B. 18, 20
Gale, J. 64
Galletly, T. W. 58
Galpin, J. O. 35
Gamon, J. 55
Gannaway, A. W. 48

Gardner, R. G. 42
Gardner, T. 76
Gardner, W. E. 22
Garle, J. L. 75
Garner, F. E. 12
Garnons-Williams, G. A. 68
Gaskell, A. B. 51
Gates, G. 24
Gay, W. 34
Geddes, A. L. 60
Gemmell, G. 59
George, P. E. 45
George, R. A. 15
Gerrard, T. F. N. 31
Gething, F. H. 52
Gibbon, C. J. 7
Gibbs, V. R. 40
Gibson, N. J. 62
Giddy, O. C. H. 78
Gill, G. 31
Gilmour, C. 52
Gilpin, G. R. P. 52
Glaisby, L. N. 35
Glanville, P. P. 70
Gledhill, J. B. 43
Glen, J. A. 51, 55
Goble, S. J. 18
Godfrey, J. D. 2
Godfrey, J. R. 49
Goldspink, H. J. 17
Good, F. H. 18
Goolden, M. 6
Gordon, E. (RNR) 30
Gordon, E. (BMM) 35
Gordon, H. P. 5
Gorley, W. J. 71
Gow, R. W. 22
Gower, H. 31
Gowney, D. J. 3
Graham, A. G. 77
Graham, J. A. 19
Grahame, R. 18, 23
Grange, E. R. 19
Grant, A. 45
Grant, G. G. 3
Grant, J. W. 15, 37
Gray, G. H. C. 31, 51
Grayston, E. T. 75
Green, H. W. 23
Green, J. R. 4
Greenwood, G. H. 67
Gregg, B. E. P. 52
Greig, A. B. 14
Gretton, P. W. 79
Grey, E. J. 61
Griffin, E. A. 49
Griffiths, H. F. 75

John, H. 40
Johnson, E. B. 18
Johnson, F. R. 40
Johnson, H. 32
Johnson, W. C. 24
Johnston, E. G. 47
Johnston, H. D. 12
Johnstone, W. A. 49
Jones, E. 59
Jones, G. H. L. 62
Jones, H. 30
Jones, J. 7
Jones, J. C. 33
Jones, J. F. 38
Jones, L. J. P. 78
Jones, T. J. 75
Jordan, W. L. 44, 47
Joyce, B. R. 19
Joyce, H. O. 3, 49
Joynson, R. 68

Keeble, N. 22
Keeley, H. P. 53
Keirstead, R. McN. 44
Keith, A. 59
Kelly, E. E. 61
Kelly, F. S. 16
Kelly, J. C. 36
Kelsey, M. H. A. 73
Kennington, S. C. 39
Kenny, A. 28
Kent, B. R. G. 18
Kerby, H. S. 38
Kerr, B. 73
Kerr, J. 31
Kerr, J. 33
Kerr, T. 11
Kerry, J. L. 21
Keslake, W. 40
Kewish, W. H. 67
Keyes, T. H. 24
Kime, J. 31
King, A. M. 32
King, C. A. 28
King, C. R. 55
King, E. W. 48, 76
King, J. A. 69
King, J. G. 15
King, W. E. H. 78
King, W. J. 28
King, W. T. 35
King-Harman, R. D. 21, 77
Kinkead, S. M. 44, 52
Kinnier, D. R. 3
Kippins, T. 54
Kirkaldy, P. 23
Kirkham, J. A. 45

Kirkpatrick, K. C. 62
Kirkwood, M. S. 58
Kitson, J. F. B. 43
Klugh, H. 49
Knight, A. V. 58
Knowles, D. 52
Knowles, F. H. 64

Ladley, G. 64
Lake, H. N. 41
Lamb, E. H. 8
Lambert, D. 72
Lambert, F. J. 57
Lambert, H. R. 10
Lamont, A. 13
Lamplough, C. R. W. 58
Lancaster, H. J. 10
Lane, F. J. 23
Lane, T. 43
Lanktree, T. F. 15
Lansley, A. 15
Lapsley, C. C. 67
Lathbury, G. P. 10
Laurenson, T. T. 30
Law, F. C. 10
Law, J. G. 8
Lawrence, J. H. 54
Lawrence, R. W. 4
Lawrie, J. 19, 37
Lawton, D. 34
Le Mésurier, T. F. 22, 35, 56
Le Patourel, C. F. 30
Leask, W. 52
Leckie, R. 29
Lee, A. B. 76
Lee, A. M. 63
Lee, J. 40
Lee, L. J. 57
Lefroy, F. C. B. 53
Legge, H. C. 77
Legh, J. A. P. 61
Leleu, H. J. 23
Lemon, S. 6
Leslie, G. 33
Leslie, N. 43
Leslie, R. F. S. 31
Lewes, A. P. M. 30
Lewis, E. R. 65
Lewis, J. 59
Lightoller, C. H. 24, 67
Liley, W. E. 70
Lilley, R. H. 7
Lillie, W. P. 59
Linaker, R. 15
Lincoln, H. 36
Litré, L. T. 9
Little, R. A. 20, 29

Littledale, B. J. 78
Llewellyn, A. P. 32
Llewellyn, I. D. 35
Lloyd, M. C. H. 12, 59
Lobb, W. 55
Lockhart, A. B. 17
Lockyer, W. R. 45
Lofthouse, F. S. 16
Logan, R. 43
Long, W. (Gnr.) 6
Long, W. (Eng. Lt.) 57
Loughlin, D. 11
Louth, T. 78
Loveless, L. S. 13, 37
Lowe, E. 1
Lower, C. 70
Lowery, J. H. 71
Lowthian, T. D. 23
Lucas-Shadwell, W. N. 53
Lupton, C. R. 42, 55
Lydekker, G. O. 53
Lyndon, G. W. H. 30
Lyon, M. 74
Lyte, F. W. 7
Lyttelton, S. C. 17

MacArthur, C. G. 7
MacCallum, F. A. 71
Macdonald, H. C. 77
Macey, J. S. 30
MacGregor, I. G. 71
Macgregor, N. M. 44
Mack, H. L. 52
Mack, R. V. 67
Mackay, H. R. 28
Mackay, J. 28
Mackenzie, A. J. 43
Mackenzie, P. H. 53
Mackenzie, R. E. F. McQ. 54
Mackenzie, W. R. 32, 35
Mackie, A. C. 60
MacKinnon, N. S. 43
MacKintosh, L. D. 69
Mackintosh, W. R. 15
Mackness, G. J. 37
MacLaurin, C. 37
MacLean, A. 71
Maclean, J. E. B. 28
MacLennan, E. S. 34
MacMillan, J. 35
MacMullin, A. R. 11, 64
Macpherson, A. D. L. 61
MacRae, A. 39, 41
Madan, A. G. 18
Madge, E. E. 11
Magor, N. A. 41
Maguire, A. 76

Temple-West, F. E. 70
Terrell, T. 42
Terry, A. H. L. 70
Terry, H. 70
Tharrett, G. W. 70
Thatcher, C. J. 59
Thaxter, E. 21
Thévenard, L. O. E. 9
Thierry, M. A. 9
Thomas, E. 71
Thomas, F. H. 12
Thomas, R. H. 49
Thomas, R. J. 18
Thomas, W. J. 62
Thomas, W. W. 56
Thompson, A. R. 14, 18
Thompson, F. 30
Thompson, G. R. 18
Thompson, G. T. 64
Thompson, J. 23
Thompson, L. 56
Thomson, A. 70
Thomson, A. C. 79
Thomson, A. D. 30, 46
Thomson, A. E. 37
Thomson, G. 52
Thomson, G. L. 11
Thomson, G. M. C. 30
Thomson, G. S. 62
Thornley, R. R. 38
Thornton, E. C. 45
Thorold, H. K. 14
Thorrowgood, W. W. 6
Tierney, T. 8
Tinmouth, W. 45
Todd, C. A. 75
Tomkins, W. J. 49
Tose, I. B. 40
Tower, I. B. B. 6
Townsley, J. W. 61
Travers, H. G. 28
Trenance, J. 49
Trendall, T. W. 3
Trickey, J. 18
Truckle, F. A. 66
Tudway, L. C. P. 11
Tufnell, D. N. C. 14
Tugwood, J. P. 19
Tulloch, R. 30
Turnbull, R. J. 28
Turner, G. R. 41
Turner, H. 22
Turner, T. 30
Turrell, J. 46
Tweedie, F. 11
Twyman, I. M. 7

Uncles, H. 21
Underhill, G. 58
Underhill, W. 52
Unsworth, G. 19
Upton, H. L. 31
Uren, F. 13
Urquhart, P. 40
Usher, R. J. 45

Varley, C. H. 37
Vaughan, P. R. 6
Vaux, P. E. 57
Venning, W. H. 3
Verey, D. R. 74
Vermulen, C. 43
Vicary, H. L. 65
Vooght, E. 49

Wainwright, A. E. 14
Waistell, A. M. 44
Walker, A. 54
Walker, C. B. 36
Walker, C. J. 18
Walker, F. W. 37
Walker, G. 30
Walker, S. M. 17
Wallace, D. 20
Waller, J. M. 54
Wallis, J. A. 56
Walls, T. A. 3
Walters, C. W. 31
Ward, M. W. 69
Ward, S. B. 31
Wardell-Yerburgh, A. 51
Warder, L. C. 20
Wardle, T. F. J. L. 1
Warne-Browne, T. A. 50
Warner, G. H. 74
Warner, W. E. 69
Warner, W. P. 45
Warwick, B. 70
Waters, A. 15
Watney, B. G. 75
Watson, J. 31, 39
Watt, A. 15
Watt, D. A. MacK. 62
Watters, E. B. 49
Watterson, T. A. 37
Waugh, J. K. 52
Webber, S. 32
Webster, D. L. 48
Webster, G. A. P. 53
Webster, R. P. D. 36
Welchman, A. W. E. 77
Weller, B. G. 16
Wellman, E. E. 55
Wells, A. H. 70

Welman, E. P. 37
Welsh, W. L. 51
West, S. G. 58
Westgarth, W. A. 49
Westwater, J. S. 21
Wharton, W. S. 14, 20
Whatling, A. O. 54
Whealy, A. T. 51, 56
Wheelwright, J. S. 37
White, A. A. 71
White, D. F. 69
White, F. W. 39
White, I. W. G. 75
White, J. P. 51
White, S. P. R. 20, 24, 37
Whitefield, J. 62
Whitehead, L. 62
Whitehead, W. 40
Whitehouse, G. T. 49
Whitmore, F. H. 32
Wiggins, E. T. 41
Wigglesworth, H. E. P. 21
Wight, R. L. 76
Wightman, H. G. E. 14
Wikner, R. L. 19
Wilkins, L. H. 52
Wilkinson, E. 30
Willett, B. R. 55
William-Powlett, N. J. W. 17
Williams, A. M. 6
Williams, L. W. 24
Williams, W. J. 37
Williams, W. T. S. 28
Williamson, A. R. 62
Willis, F. E. 30
Willm, E. D. 9
Wills, T. H. 75
Wilson, C. T. 36
Wilson, H. 74
Wilson, H. M. 6
Wilson, J. P. 4
Wilson, W. (Skpr) 52
Wilson, W. (Lt) 62
Wilson, W. H. 52
Wilton, G. 52
Wink, F. 10
Witten, E. 40
Wollaston, A. F. R. 43
Wood, C. 70
Wood, G. 72
Wood, H. H. 49
Wood, J. G. 18
Wood, J. H. A. 36
Wood, T. G. C. 37
Wood, W. (648SA) 23
Wood, W. (2551SA) 48
Wood, W. F. 55

www.ingramcontent.com/pod-product-compliance
Lightning Source LLC
Chambersburg PA
CBHW081154090426
42736CB00017B/3325